THE BLACK EYED premiered at Magic Theater
(Chris Smith, Artistic Director; David Gluck, Managing
Director) on 14 May 2005. The cast and creative
contributors were as follows:

AIESHA .... Nora el Samahy
TAMAM .... Bridgette Loriaux
THE ARCHITECT .... Atosa Babaoff
DELILAH .... Sofia Ahmad

Director .... Jessica Heidt
Set design .... Kris Stone
Lighting design .... Chris Studley
Sound design .... D Schultz
Costume design .... Callie Floor
Production stage manager .... Leslie Grisdale

The play opened in Athens, Greece at Fournos Theatre
on 25 April 2007. The cast and creative contributors
were as follows:

AIESHA .... Anna Koutsaftiki
TAMAM .... Evdokia Statiri
THE ARCHITECT .... Kalliroe Miriagou
DELILAH .... Stevi Fortoma

Director .... Takis Tzamargias
Translation .... Athina Paraponiari
Set & costume design .... Kostis Davaris
Sound design .... Platon Andritsakis

The play opened off-Broadway at New York Theater Workshop (James C Nicola, Artistic Director; Lynn Moffat, Managing Director) on 31 July 2007. The cast and creative contributors were as follows:

AIESHA . . . . Aysan Celik
TAMAM . . . . Lameece Issaq
THE ARCHITECT . . . . Jeanine Serralles
DELILAH . . . . Emily Swallow

Director . . . . Sam Gold
Set design . . . . Paul Steinberg
Lighting design . . . . Jane Cox
Sound design . . . . Darron L West
Costume design . . . . Gabriel Berry
Production stage manager . . . . Rachel Zack

CHARACTERS & SETTING

AIESHA, *a woman*
TAMAM, *a woman*
THE ARCHITECT, *a woman*
DELILAH, *a woman*

The stage is very sparse.

AUTHOR'S NOTE

It is indicated in the text where the characters speak as part of a chorus.

INTRODUCTION

The point of publishing a preface to a play, particularly
when written by its author, is to seduce readers
into making the commitment to turn the page and
experience the work itself. By putting into print
lofty proclamations about your intentions and the
motivating factors that compelled you to write a
particular work, you are teasing your readers, hoping
to excite within them a desire to see if you succeeded in
doing what you set out to do. Again, it's about getting
them to begin at the real beginning.

I myself love authors' introductions. They feel as if they
are addressed to young writers or at least that it how
I usually experience them. Tennessee Williams'
introduction to A STREETCAR NAMED DESIRE,
first published as an essay entitled *The Catastrophe of
Success*, is a piece of writing that I often find myself
rereading and recommending to my students. Picking
up his introduction on a Sunday morning in the
summer of 2000 would change the course of my
playwriting career. It would help me begin the journey
I needed to take before I could produce a play like
THE BLACK EYED, a work in which I tried to capture
the complexity of being a Palestinian-American woman
living in New York in the wake of September 11.

Tennessee's introduction, a meditation on how external
validation can give an artist no pleasure that compares
with the satisfaction of creation, has little to do with
the play itself. It can stand alone as an essay, but it

shouldn't. By that, I mean, Tennessee's declarations on how money/fame/adulation can never provide lasting joy are much more fascinating because it is he—the man capable of writing THE GLASS MENAGERIE and A STREETCAR NAMED DESIRE—who is making them.

In 2000, I had graduated from the Yale School of Drama and was in the process of making my big move back to New York in the hopes of becoming a professional theatre artist. I had begun writing plays in high school and had written several by the time I got to Yale. One of my first works was a one-act written in blank verse in which Shakespeare's tragic characters come to life in order to harass him into changing the endings of their stories. I mention this to highlight that, from my earliest days as a writer, I wrote plays that dealt with my ethnic identity and plays that did not. I continued to do so in graduate school, but I chose not to have my plays that dealt with Arab-American themes produced. I didn't want to be pigeonholed. I had seen what usually happened to writers of color and I didn't like it one bit. Initially, a colorful playwright gets perhaps a bit more attention and has access to a few more grants, but— over the course of a career—it seemed that it was the writers who were seen as "truly" American who were being sustained. Their work was viewed as universal.

I wanted to be smart about my career choices. Though I never denied my ethnic heritage when questioned about it, I decided to allow the "reality" of how the current American playwriting market seemed to work become an influence on which plays I would let the world see first and which plays I would keep to myself. Until I had made a name for myself in the theater. Until I felt safe, which is hard to feel when you're in your early twenties anyway, particularly if you are a

minority trying to break into a field where few or no
members of your race are working.

Of course I also knew that, if I produced my plays that
dealt with my ethnic identity first, I would have to talk
about my personal and family history, which has been
very much shaped by the Palestinian-Israeli conflict.
Why tackle a subject as polarizing and controversial as
the modern Middle East? Especially if you enjoy being
well-liked as much as I do? The answer, of course,
is that you absolutely should not. Unless you have to.

September 11 would change how I as an
Arab-American was seen, but it was picking up
A STREETCAR NAMED DESIRE and rereading its
introduction, only about a year before that tragedy
occurred, that would change how I saw the seminal
works of American theatre. It would also change how
I thought about what might be my place in American
theatre if I was brave enough to try.

I have never been good at unpacking boxes of books,
because it is hard for me to put books on a shelf without
feeling the need to reread one of them immediately. On
that day, I picked up A STREETCAR NAMED DESIRE
and promised myself that I'd only read the last line of
Tennessee's brilliant introduction before I went back
to unpacking. That line, in which Tennessee writes that
"the monosyllable of the clock is loss, loss, loss unless
you devote your life to its opposition", had become a
sort of mantra for me. Of course, my mantra convinced
me that it would be a loss, loss, loss to spend my
morning unpacking when I felt consumed with the
desire to reread my favorite American play instead.
So, I delved into the world of Blanche DuBois. She was
a character that reminded me of many of the powerful,
sharp Arab women that I had known (too) well all
my life. Women who loved sex and tried to pretend
otherwise in order to get the affection of men. Women

who were unpleasant house-guests, who had a particular combination of being mindnumbingly entitled and heartbreakingly vulnerable that made them so easy to destroy.

Up to that point, I had viewed Tennessee Williams as a white writer, but I realized then that his best work always seemed tied to his very specific cultural identity. Southern American writers who wrote about their culture were illuminating a subset of our society that felt as distinct and specific as African-American or Arab-American culture. I, like too many American theatergoers and academics, just chose not to see it that way. I had fallen into the trap of viewing the world of American writers as either white or not white, universal or limited, "us" or "them." I then picked up a few of the plays I had written in graduate school (yes, it took me months to unpack). It quickly became clear that the plays that dealt directly with my ethnic heritage were my best works thus far and that I had to start trying to get them produced. I realized I could write not only *despite* by fear of being pigeonholed, but also *about* my fear of being pigeonholed and of having my opportunities limited because of who I was.

CHOCOLATE IN HEAT and ROAR were my first works that were produced in New York, and ROAR became the first play by a Palestinian-American playwright to premiere off-Broadway. Both were plays that I had written, but never shown to anyone in their entirety, while I was a graduate student. Though they were about the Arab-American immigrant experience and had exclusively Arab-American characters in them, they did not deal directly with the Middle East conflict. THE BLACK EYED is my first play that does.

I began working on THE BLACK EYED right after September 11. Because it is an extremely political and non-linear play written in free verse with a chorus,

I half-believed I would never find a major producer
willing to take it on and that freed me to write in a way
I had not attempted to write before. It's a cliche to say
that your best work as an artist happens when you
aren't trying to please anyone but yourself, but I don't
think it is an accident that THE BLACK EYED was
my first play to have multiple productions and be
translated into different languages.

Having this play produced in Greece was one of
the nicest things that ever happened to me, perhaps
because it required the least amount of development
of any of my previous productions. All I did was hand
a script to a Greek actress whom I had met by chance,
telling her, "I think Greek audiences might dig this
play. It has a chorus." Less than a year later I was being
flown to Athens for its opening. I expected the Greek
producer and artists involved to be highly politicized
and informed about Middle Eastern politics. But, the
questions that the director and actors had for me were
all about the play's structure and the characters' specific
personality traits. After a bit of ouzo on opening night,
I took the producer aside and asked her why she felt
it was important to do a play about four Palestinian
women in Greece. She looked slightly surprised at my
question. Then, she said that she never really thought
about the play as being about four Palestinians. She
said she thought the story was about four strong people.

Enough teasing. I hope you will enjoy THE BLACK
EYED.

to my much-loved and loving parents,
Charles and Ghada Shamieh,
who always made the improbable seem possible

(AIESHA *is alone on-stage, facing the audience.*)

AIESHA: Unanswered questions,
Unquestioned answers.
I do someone good dead.
I do someone dead good.
What is the point of the revolution that begins with
the little hand?
Any little hand?
(*Lifts her right hand and looks at it*) This little hand?
Unanswered questions,
Unquestioned answers—

(ARCHITECT, DELILAH, *and* TAMAM *enter. They do not
notice* AIESHA *at first.*)

TAMAM: (*Points towards the audience*) There's the door!

(*The three women then see* AIESHA.)

DELILAH: (*To* AIESHA) We heard a rumor.
We heard that all the martyrs
were sitting in the one room
in the afterlife.

ARCHITECT: (*Points towards the audience*)
The one right there!

TAMAM: The room no one knows anything about, the
room no one but martyrs have dared to go in.

DELILAH: And no one who goes in

ARCHITECT: comes out.

CHORUS: (ARCHITECT, DELILAH & TAMAM)
Should we believe it?

(Pause. AIESHA *looks at each woman carefully before she finally speaks.)*

AIESHA: Tell me who you are.

CHORUS: (ARCHITECT, DELILAH & TAMAM)
And you'll know who we're looking for?

TAMAM: My name is Tamam.
It means enough.
I need to see the thing that started out smaller than me
and got bigger.
I need to see my brother.

DELILAH: Women were his only weakness.
I was his only woman.
They called me Delilah.
I'm here for Samson.

(Pause)

TAMAM: *(To* ARCHITECT*)* Answer her questions, girl.
She may help us.
(To AIESHA*)* I don't know her name.

ARCHITECT: I'm the architect
of the unseen, underlying structures,
the buildings that have never been built.

TAMAM: I don't know who she's looking for.

ARCHITECT: I'm here for answers from the only one
who can give them to me.

CHORUS: (ARCHITECT, DELILAH & TAMAM) Let us in.

AIESHA: Go right ahead.
(Motions towards the audience)
The door is unlocked. *(Pause)*
Afraid? Tell me why and I'll tell you if you have good
reason to be.

(ARCHITECT, DELILAH, *and* TAMAM, *all begin speaking at once.)*

DELILAH: *(Overlapping)* Women were his only
weakness, and I was his only woman.

TAMAM: *(Overlapping)* Started out smaller than me and
got bigger. I want to see my brother.

ARCHITECT: *(Overlapping)* He passed me and knew I
was an Arab.

AIESHA: Hold on!
Women and weakness?
You'll speak first.

DELILAH: Women were his only weakness
And I was his only woman.

CHORUS: (ARCHITECT & TAMAM) Yeah, right.

DELILAH:
Okay, the only one that mattered. And I asked—

CHORUS: (ARCHITECT & TAMAM) Will you have me?
Do you want me?
Do you love me?

DELILAH: I asked him—
What makes your strength weak?
Show me the crack in your armor, so I may lick and seal
it together.
Let me keep you safe from
those who hate you and wish you dead.

AIESHA: So you refused to put out till he told you, right?
Crudeness is necessary for clarity.

DELILAH: Basically.

CHORUS: (ARCHITECT & TAMAM)
It comes down to the basics.
You knew the only power
you had over men was sexual.

AIESHA: Those were your means.

DELILAH: I used them.

AIESHA: You acted justly, Delilah.
You saved your people.

DELILAH: My people!
My people called me a whore.
I overheard a young man from my own clan say.

CHORUS: (ARCHITECT & TAMAM)
The whore did her job and she did it well.

DELILAH: He didn't call me
the daughter of an honorable man,
or a good woman who loved her people—

CHORUS: (AIESHA, ARCHITECT & TAMAM)
but a whore.

DELILAH: But not at first
No, not...of course.
The elders came to me after my brother died.
They knew I was alone,
they knew I intended to stay that way.

AIESHA: So they made you seduce Samson?
They forced you into it?

DELILAH: Worse.
They made me think it was my idea.
They asked me to take my father's place at their meetings,
even though I was a girl,
because my only brother was dead.
We talked of many things.
They listened as if my opinions mattered,
as if I mattered.
They were polite.

CHORUS: (ARCHITECT & TAMAM) Too polite.

DELILAH: I told them my ideas about how to prevent
the cattle from dying and why our well always ran dry.
Out of the blue, my father's best friend brought up

Samson.
We rarely talked about Samson in our villages.

CHORUS: (ARCHITECT & TAMAM)
The problems that are the most pressing

DELILAH: are the ones you tend to ignore.
He stated the obvious.
He said if Samson isn't stopped

CHORUS: (ARCHITECT, DELILAH & TAMAM)
It won't matter whether we have enough to eat next
season.

DELILAH:
My father's friend said our men can't win against him.
We don't want to lose more men like your unparalleled
brother,
your brother with a face like the moon.

TAMAM: I want to see my brother.

AIESHA: Let the girl tell her story.

DELILAH:
He said the only weakness that man has is for women.
And then in perfect time, they all turned and looked at
me.
It was then that I offered to try.

AIESHA: You offered?!

DELILAH:
I should have known by the way they were talking
that they wanted something from me.
And they sure knew how to get it.
My father's closest friend took me aside after the
meeting,
as if he had a secret to share about my father.
But all he told me was what my father himself told me
often enough,

CHORUS: (ARCHITECT & TAMAM)
If I had known I could make daughters like you, Delilah,
I would have wished for a dozen.

DELILAH: Their words were honey.
Sweet,

CHORUS: (ARCHITECT & TAMAM)
without substance in heat.

DELILAH: Everyone thought I did it,
because my brother had been killed by Samson in the
last battle.
My brother was the first of a hundred men to charge at
Samson.
Being in the front was dangerous,
almost suicide.

CHORUS: (AIESHA, ARCHITECT & TAMAM) Suicide!

DELILAH: Only fools fought in the front,
but someone had to be a fool
if there was to be a fight at all.
Samson snatched up my brother first.
but killed him last.
He made a game of dangling him,
choking him in the crook of his arm,
while he
with his other iron fist
continued to knock the heads off the necks
of all my cousins, neighbors, and friends.

ARCHITECT: Hands change!

DELILAH: (Ignoring the ARCHITECT's outburst)
Not only everyone you loved,
but everyone you knew,

CHORUS: (AIESHA, DELILAH & TAMAM) lost someone.

DELILAH: A wife of a man killed charged at Samson,
roaring, livid, full of a uniquely female fury

that when you witness
makes you sure
this woman can punch through a wall,
kill a lion if it chanced on her path,
till a man flattens her with a half-of-his-strength hit.

AIESHA: He hit her?

DELILAH: That would be tacky.
Samson was a lot of things, but he wasn't tacky.
He grabbed her and kissed her passionately.
and she scratched and bit and pushed at him,
he told her

CHORUS: (ARCHITECT, DELILAH & TAMAM)
"I like 'em kinky."

DELILAH:
It was then that I saw my brother was not moving.

AIESHA: Now your story makes sense.
You're here to see your brother.

DELILAH: I am not here to see my brother.

TAMAM: My brother!
Have you seen him?
He looks like me,
Black hair, black [eyes]—

AIESHA: Hold your horses, Tamar!

TAMAM: It's Tamam.

AIESHA: Whatever.
(To DELILAH)
So who are you here to see?

DELILAH: I told you before. Samson.

AIESHA: To spit in his face, right?

DELILAH: He might kind of dig that, but no.

CHORUS: (ARCHITECT & TAMAM) Gross.

DELILAH: That's my Samson. He's quite special.

AIESHA: How did you wrench from him the secret of
where his power lied?

DELILAH:
You mean, what's so bewitching about little ole me?
I'm a pretty woman.
It's not a boast,

CHORUS: (ARCHITECT & TAMAM) it's a fact.

AIESHA: But pretty enough to die to have?

DELILAH: But you want to know precisely
what he loved about me,
so you'll understand why he told me his dark secret.
Do you want to know why he put the power of his fate
in the nest of my interlaced hands?

AIESHA:
Obviously I want to know. I already asked you, bitch.

DELILAH: What does it matter?
What good does it do for you to know?
We're all dead.
There's no hope of using the knowledge to seduce.

CHORUS: (AIESHA, ARCHITECT & TAMAM)
But it can't hurt.

DELILAH:
Women, what do you do when you want a man?
This is what I did and this is what I suggest.
Go to where he frequents.
Dress well, dress in a way that makes it obvious you are
a (Pause) woman.

CHORUS: (ARCHITECT & TAMAM)
Men can never tell the difference
between a beautiful woman

DELILAH: and a person dressed like one.
He'll take you,

because you're there and available.
Then, he'll probably leave you alone,
like Samson did to me,
immediately and for days, weeks, months, years.

CHORUS: (ARCHITECT & TAMAM)
Or did it just feel that way?

DELILAH: Either way, the waiting killed me. What's the
difference between a thing that feels like it kills you and
the one that actually does?

AIESHA: Plenty,
but go on.

DELILAH: I almost went back to my people,
gave up.
But then one morning,
I opened my door and there he was, about to knock.
He didn't say hello. He just announced,

CHORUS: (ARCHITECT & TAMAM)
"You can live with me for a while."

DELILAH: ...and I said, "Yes, I can."
I didn't know that there would be his other lovers
living there too,
all Philistine women,
like myself.
I had never met any of them before. They were poor
girls.
At home, we did not run in the same circles. Do you
understand?

CHORUS: (ARCHITECT & TAMAM) We understand.

DELILAH: I was surprised, my pride was wounded.
But I thought to myself,

CHORUS: (ARCHITECT, DELILAH & TAMAM)
"I am in the process of erasing you

DELILAH: I will watch you cower and then crumble
into dust before me."

CHORUS: (ARCHITECT, DELILAH & TAMAM)
You will pay for every pleasure you exact from my pain.

DELILAH:
Believe that and it's surprisingly easy not to be jealous.
My indifference made me different
so he began to prefer me.

CHORUS: (ARCHITECT & TAMAM)
"Preference" is the first domino of human feeling.

DELILAH: Hit it hard, and it knocks over "like", "need",
and finally

CHORUS: (ARCHITECT & TAMAM) "love".

DELILAH: I need to go inside.

TAMAM: Go, I'll follow.

DELILAH: I should.
(Motions towards the audience)
He's in there. I know it. It's like I can feel him watching
me.
(Addresses the audience as if she sees Samson)
Samson!
I begged my people not to hurt you.
They promised, I almost believed.
When they blinded you, I could not see,
how to show you though I loved my people more,

CHORUS: (ARCHITECT, DELILAH & TAMAM)
I still loved you.

DELILAH: Surrounded by darkness, I knew you,
who loved me without lights on,
would recognize

CHORUS: (ARCHITECT, DELILAH & TAMAM) my touch.

DELILAH: I touched, muttering a skeleton of apologies.
You sliced through the bone saying,

CHORUS: (ARCHITECT & TAMAM)
"Leave! Your presence torments me."

DELILAH: I stayed, you cursed me.
I fled your cries and the cruelty you learned from me.
Outside, looking in,
I saw you framed in the doorway
of that great hall that stood so tall.

CHORUS: (ARCHITECT, DELILAH & TAMAM)
that seemed only God's hand could make fall.

DELILAH: You, with your head cocked as you watched
me with your ears.
Your arms stretched out
The pillars exploded.

CHORUS: (ARCHITECT & TAMAM) The world went flat.

DELILAH: You spared me.
Your people dug and found you
under the layers of mine.
I prayed that you would rest softly in their soil.
I wished your God could have kept you safe

CHORUS: (ARCHITECT, DELILAH & TAMAM)
from she who loved you,

DELILAH: but still wished you dead.

AIESHA: Nice story. But I don't suggest you stick to it.

DELILAH: Why not?

AIESHA: Trust me, you won't be welcome in there if you
tell that story.

DELILAH: How do you know?

AIESHA: Maybe because I've been in there.

TAMAM: What? Really? Did you see my brother?

AIESHA: I wouldn't know him if I did.

TAMAM: How did you get in? Why did you leave?

AIESHA: It's a long story.

DELILAH: I don't believe you. No one who goes into that room comes out.

AIESHA: Don't believe me. Go in. Tell your story. See what happens.

DELILAH: If it's true you went in
why didn't you stay?

AIESHA: Like I said, it's a long story.

ARCHITECT: Why is everybody always talking about length? There are other factors to consider.

(Pause)

AIESHA: What?

TAMAM: Excuse her. She's not very articulate.

DELILAH: You'll get used to her.

TAMAM: She means to ask why do people mention the length of a *story* as a reason not to tell it?

DELILAH:
When there are far more important factors to consider—like how badly we need to know it.

AIESHA: Okay.
It's not a long story, it's a very short one and it ends with a real bang.

ARCHITECT: Hands change!

AIESHA: I ask the questions.
How long have you been together?

CHORUS: *(ARCHITECT, DELILAH & TAMAM)* A long time.

TAMAM: Not long enough to hate one another,

DELILAH: but long enough to know

CHORUS: (ARCHITECT, DELILAH & TAMAM)
we eventually will.

TAMAM: Please try to remember if you've seen my brother.
He was about this tall *(Frantically indicates a height that would suggest a tall man)* and had—

AIESHA: What was his name?

TAMAM: Muhammed.

AIESHA: Muhammed? Do you know how many Muhammeds are probably in there?

TAMAM: No more than there are Johns.

AIESHA: True.

CHORUS: (ARCHITECT, DELILAH & TAMAM)
(Speaking together as if chanting a prayer)
Help us take our first step towards that room.

TAMAM: Water goes from solid to liquid,

ARCHITECT: people don't just cease.

DELILAH: Our loved ones are allowed an afterlife,

TAMAM: just like every other misguided soul who murdered and raped.

DELILAH: Some of our martyrs were mistaken,

ARCHITECT: cruel,

TAMAM: even insane.

CHORUS: (ARCHITECT, DELILAH & TAMAM)
But the fact remains,
they are not worse than the worst of them that are here.

DELILAH: We believe in
our loved ones
who are sitting in that room in front of us.

ARCHITECT: *(Points to the audience)*
That room! And we only need to go in.

TAMAM: To see our brothers.

DELILAH: Our lovers.

ARCHITECT: Our strangers.

CHORUS: (ARCHITECT, DELILAH & TAMAM)
We are in heaven.
And when we woke up here,

ARCHITECT: there was a mint on the pillow
beside the one we slept on
and a note that had fallen off the bed.

TAMAM: The note said:

CHORUS: (ARCHITECT, DELILAH & TAMAM)
Welcome to heaven,
where everything you believe to be true is true.

(The prayer ends.)

ARCHITECT: But we can't control what we believe.

TAMAM: That's what makes our heaven such hell.

DELILAH: I don't care. I want to see Samson. I'm sure
they'll welcome me in the martyr's room when they
know how much I love him.

AIESHA: If you believe that, I've got a peace process I
can sell you.

ARCHITECT: *(To* AIESHA*)* What's your name?

AIESHA: Aiesha.

ARCHITECT:
You look so familiar. Do I look familiar to you?

AIESHA: No.

ARCHITECT: Were you famous?

AIESHA: Yes, but you wouldn't know me.

ARCHITECT: Maybe I do. When were you alive?

AIESHA: Listen, half-wit. I said you didn't.
You speak out of turn again and I'll make you go stand
with one of the other groups of women that are around
here.
But they probably won't have you either, so you'll be
all alone.
You want to be alone?

ARCHITECT: *(Looking at* TAMAM *and* AIESHA*)* But...

AIESHA: Don't look at your friends. Keep looking at me.
They're not going to help you.

TAMAM: We have to do what she says.

DELILAH: She may get us in the room.

TAMAM: Don't be difficult!

AIESHA: They know I'm right.
Look at me and answer my questions.
Do you want to be alone?

(The ARCHITECT *shakes her head.)*

AIESHA: Listen, you worthless waste of a human soul.
I'm going to ask you again—do I look familiar?

ARCHITECT: Yes, but—

*(*AIESHA *approaches her, menacing.)*

ARCHITECT: No.

AIESHA: That's what I thought.

DELILAH: What you think, we think.

TAMAM: You're certainly not a religious figure.

AIESHA: What makes you say that?

TAMAM: Maybe you are, but I didn't read about you
when I scoured the Holy Books of every religion that
ever existed. Looking for a trace of what all the world

religions say happens to martyrs, so I can figure out
where my brother might be.
Do you think you can go in and ask about him now?
If you wouldn't mind...

DELILAH: Forget her brother. You'll notice Samson. He's
the big guy. He'll probably hit on you. Tell him to come
out and get me.

TAMAM:
I knew I should never have let you follow me here.

DELILAH: I didn't follow you! I've looked at all those
books too. I did just as much work as you did to get
here.

TAMAM: You were wandering.
You saw that this girl *(Points to the* ARCHITECT*)* was
following me.
At least she stays quiet, except when she screams
something about hands and change.

ARCHITECT: Hands change!

TAMAM: Like that.
I went to talk to all the gods and prophets
of all the religions that ever were.
They tried their best to tell us where to locate the
martyrs in the after-life.
None had a clue, except this god that humans prayed to
before they made it to the sapien part of the homo
sapien.

ARCHITECT: It was at the homo erectus point in the
chain of human development.

DELILAH: Homo erectus?

TAMAM: You'd know that if you did the research.

DELILAH: Okay, I didn't do all the research you did.
I just stood around and said,
(Flirty) "I need a little information.

Does anyone want to help me out?"
Then this monkey-like god appeared,
ready to, you know, help out.

TAMAM: What was this monkey god's name?

DELILAH: Oo-oo-oo is what he called himself.

TAMAM: I can't believe Oo-oo-oo told you where he
thought the martyrs might be.

DELILAH: What's the big deal?

TAMAM: Oo-oo-oo told me I was the only person he
was going to tell.

DELILAH: Well, if it makes you feel better, it wasn't easy
to get it out of him. It took a lot of persuasion.

TAMAM: You persuaded him too?

AIESHA: You're obviously pretty good at persuasion,
Delilah.

DELILAH: It has been said that I am.
I got him drunk on banana wine, and I had my share
too.
Then he began to talk.
He said—
(Mimics Oo-oo-oo for the next section in quotes)
"Look, I'm going to get into trouble for telling you this.
I don't like to mess with the martyrs.
No one does. But there was this room at the corner of
heaven,
where the columbus monkeys who sacrifice themselves

AIESHA: who run towards the predators

DELILAH: so their loved ones have time to get away,

AIESHA: Who run towards their predators
so the weaker ones aren't certain prey.

DELILAH: They used to hang out in this room, long
before humans were invented.

We gods have talked and we figured out this is the
place where the human martyrs must be too."
That's the story he tells if you persuade him enough.

TAMAM: Yes.
But banana wine is cheap and persuading a monkey is
easier than you might think.
The Monkey God obviously likes all kinds of women.

AIESHA: That's right. Women of all different cultures
and all centuries
have come here to look for their martyrs.

CHORUS: (ARCHITECT, DELILAH & TAMAM)
They get stuck here, too stubborn to give up searching,

AIESHA: too afraid to go in.

*(In the following dialogue, each woman points to different
areas of the stage to indicate the different groups of women.)*

DELILAH: There must be the Japanese women, whose
men kamikazied their way here and haven't been seen
since.

TAMAM: Over there are Iranian mothers, who helped
convince their children it was their duty to run through
land riddled with land mines.

DELILAH: Here are the Tamil women, sisters of the
Black Tigers who sit for centuries,

ARCHITECT: waiting.

DELILAH: There! Those are the Buddhists,
mostly mothers of monks who made love to fire
and died in its embrace.

ARCHITECT: The Irish girls are over there,
whose fathers starved themselves in the hope of tasting
freedom.

AIESHA: They tend to sing to pass the time.

TAMAM: There are the Jewish ladies,
the relatives of the unsung
heroes of the Holocaust,
unnamed, because anyone who might have seen or
been told about their brave acts died almost
immediately after them.

ARCHITECT: unknown

DELILAH: except to their loved ones who will not rest
till they find them again.

CHORUS: (ARCHITECT, DELILAH & TAMAM)
There is no hatred here.
Each of us wishes each of them well.

DELILAH:
Here we wait in heaven, at the gate of the martyrs' door.
Though none of us seem to have discussed it or decided
upon it,

TAMAM:
somehow we have managed to separate ourselves
into the groups,

ARCHITECT: the races,

CHORUS: (ARCHITECT, DELILAH & TAMAM)
we identified with while we were alive.

AIESHA: So, you three are all Palestinians?

CHORUS: (ARCHITECT, DELILAH & TAMAM) Yes.

TAMAM: Even in heaven, you can breathe more easily
with your own people.

DELILAH: Here we are

TAMAM: and here we have
segregated ourselves

ARCHITECT: almost by accident.

AIESHA: All except for her.

DELILAH: Philistine is how you pronounce Palestine in Arabic in my day and in yours, Aiesha. You know that.

AIESHA: All I know is that you like kosher dick, bitch.

ARCHITECT: Ugly! No hands! Change!

TAMAM: Aiesha, I want your help.
But that kind of talk is not necessary.

AIESHA: It's not necessary to speak my mind but I'm going to do so anyway.

DELILAH: Don't worry, Tamam. I can handle her. I like men and all the different flavors they come in. And trust me, when they do come, it is in different flavors.

AIESHA: Forbidden fruit rots quickly.
You know why he liked you so much?

ARCHITECT: Oh, no!

DELILAH:
You don't know anything about what he felt for me.

AIESHA: Because, while having you,
he was able to relive murdering all your men.

ARCHITECT: Hands!

AIESHA: *(To the* ARCHITECT*)* You shut up!
(To DELILAH*)* So why don't you go join the Jewish women, Delilah?

TAMAM: Aiesha, that's enough.

DELILAH: Just because I love someone else doesn't mean I become something else.

AIESHA: Whatever.

ARCHITECT: You seem so familiar.

AIESHA: Don't you start with that again!

DELILAH: You were never in that room.

AIESHA: Yes, I was! I went in and came back out.

TAMAM: Not possible.

AIESHA: I am a martyr.
There are female martyrs too, you know.
I built something more intricate than the human heart,
hugged it to my chest,
and walked into the biggest crowd I could find...

DELILAH: How could you do that?
It's so angry.

CHORUS: (ARCHITECT, DELILAH & TAMAM)
It's so male.

AIESHA: Let's put it this way.
Oppression is like a coin maker.

TAMAM: That's what my brother said!

AIESHA: Can you keep it to yourself, Reham?
I'm trying to tell my story.
I suggest you listen to it. It may be of some interest to
you and yours.

TAMAM: Sorry. It's Tamam, by the way.

AIESHA: You should be.
Unlike some people, I didn't stand on the sidelines,
seducing my way into saving my people's skin

DELILAH: It worked.

AIESHA: Not for long.

DELILAH:
Samson only killed the Philistines in the banquet hall,
had he lived and had I not wrung his secret from him,
he would have slaughtered us all.
Check your sources, remember who wrote them.
If you do, angry woman, you might find out
you're closer to me than you think.
I might be your ancestor.

AIESHA: We've heard enough out of you.
Go hang out with the Jewish women.

DELILAH: Religion doesn't mean anything here.
I was born before your religion even existed.
(To the ARCHITECT *and* TAMAM*)*
Let's go speak with those Iranian mothers,

CHORUS: *(*ARCHITECT *&* TAMAM*)* No.

DELILAH: Let's ask if they want to walk in with us.

AIESHA: That's a bad idea, whore.

DELILAH: Words like that don't mean anything here,
because up here we know
there isn't a woman alive who doesn't sell herself...

(Pause)

CHORUS: *(*ARCHITECT, DELILAH *&* TAMAM*)* short.

AIESHA: Maybe that's true of weak women like you,
but women like me take matters into our own hands
and we get our rewards.
The minute I got to the afterlife,
I had a hundred men of every hue.
That's what I believed I'd get.

CHORUS: *(*ARCHITECT, DELILAH *&* TAMAM*)*
So that meant that's what you got.

CHORUS: *(*ARCHITECT, DELILAH *&* TAMAM*)*
We do know that all religions are wacky

DELILAH: And if you don't buy that,

TAMAM:
You haven't read your own Book with honest eyes.

DELILAH:
Everyone picks and chooses what's convenient
about their own religion,

CHORUS: (ARCHITECT, DELILAH & TAMAM)
And should keep that in mind

AIESHA: before they start judging someone else's.
I believed my book
when it said
Heaven is indescribable in human terms

CHORUS: (ARCHITECT, DELILAH & TAMAM)
i.e. you just won't get it

AIESHA: So, to describe indescribable delight.
it said that men who live virtuously
Don't actually get to have a bunch of sexy, dark-eyed
women
But they have pleasures
that will feel like
What can only in inferior human terms
be understood as

CHORUS: (ARCHITECT, DELILAH & TAMAM)
hanging out with a bunch of *houris*,
who were hot

AIESHA: virgins whose virginity is continually renewed,
also known as

CHORUS: (AIESHA, ARCHITECT, DELILAH & TAMAM)
the Black Eyed.

AIESHA: I interpreted that to mean that if I blew myself
up and took others with me,
because no one would give a shit about my people's
plight unless I did,
I would have a hundred men of every hue.
who were lined up like fruits at the market.

CHORUS: (ARCHITECT, DELILAH & TAMAM)
Ready for the picking and the plucking.

AIESHA: Men, forever chaste with their chastity
renewing throughout eternity, untouched, eager.
I had them all.

TAMAM: In what religious text did you find that if you
blew yourself up you'd have a hundred men of every
hue?

AIESHA: Okay, my interpretation is a rather loose one.
But, hey, it's heaven.
That's what I believed, that's what I got.

ARCHITECT:
How could you leave a hundred men of every hue?

DELILAH: Did you happen to miss that she said that
these men had no
sexual experience?
How many times can a woman scream—
"That's not it.

CHORUS: (DELILAH & TAMAM) That's not near it.

DELILAH: That's so far away,

CHORUS: (DELILAH & TAMAM)
you might as well be rubbing the soles of my shoes
without them even being on my feet."

(ARCHITECT *laughs hysterically.*)

AIESHA: It isn't that funny. Why are you laughing?
(*To* TAMAM) Make her stop.

TAMAM: Actually, it is funny.
You're a pretty girl, Aiesha.
It's not a compliment. It's a fact.
And you blew yourself up
and ended up with a hundred male virgins in heaven

DELILAH: When any girl could have twice that number
on earth if she wanted to.

(*All three women laugh at* AIESHA.)

AIESHA: Shut up. Shut up.

DELILAH: And now you're hanging out with us,
because for some reason, the martyrs don't want you in
there with them.

AIESHA: I could go back there anytime.

TAMAM: Then, go!
Ask our loved ones if they want us to visit.

AIESHA: The door is unlocked.
Just walk in.
Your loved ones are in there.
Don't you think they want to see you
as much as you want to see them?

DELILAH: You go first.
Help us and we'll be in your everlasting debt.

AIESHA: Everlasting debt is overrated and hardly ever
paid in full.

TAMAM: I can't take it anymore. Go in there right now
and ask about my brother!

AIESHA: Shut up!

TAMAM: You go in there right now.

ARCHITECT: Stop fighting.

AIESHA: We're not fighting, Retard. I'm ignoring her.

TAMAM: Tell my brother I have something to say to him.
Go!

CHORUS: (ARCHITECT & DELILAH) Hold on a minute.

DELILAH: We agreed.
We're in this together.
If we're asking her to go in, she should ask about all our
loved ones.

TAMAM: No, you're going to ask about my brother first,
before you look for anyone else.

AIESHA: Heyam, I don't care about you or your stupid—

TAMAM: My name is Tamam.
It means enough.
I was called that because my family wanted

CHORUS: (ARCHITECT & DELILAH) no more daughters.

TAMAM:
I am the last of seven sisters, good luck for the family.
Because, after me, a brother was born.
The only one.

CHORUS: (ARCHITECT & DELILAH)
Why do our people rejoice when a boy child is born?

TAMAM: Because times like these call for soldiers,
to fight
the Europeans and their Holy War,
crusading against we people who lived here before,

CHORUS: (ARCHITECT, DELILAH & TAMAM)
and will live here afterwards.

TAMAM: I want to talk about something smaller than me

CHORUS: (ARCHITECT, DELILAH & TAMAM)
that became bigger.

TAMAM: I want to talk about my brother.
He was caught with a weapon in his hand
and a curse on his lips.
I went to the jail to pay a ransom for his release
Most of my people looked at the Crusaders
with every ounce of hatred a human heart can hold,
their faces twisted not like they tasted something bitter,

CHORUS: (ARCHITECT, DELILAH & TAMAM) like
something bitter was being forced down their throats.

TAMAM: I was smarter than that.
I knew I must navigate through the maze of might,
and did my best to be kindly,

CHORUS: (ARCHITECT, DELILAH & TAMAM) polite,

TAMAM: Hoping perhaps that I would
Remind them of a woman
that they knew.

CHORUS: (ARCHITECT & DELILAH)
Or would have liked to know.

TAMAM: So when they beat my brother,
that thing that started out smaller than me and became
bigger,
they would, perhaps maybe for my sake,

CHORUS: (ARCHITECT, DELILAH & TAMAM)
lighten their touch.

TAMAM: I am a pretty woman.
It's not a boast.

CHORUS: (ARCHITECT & DELILAH) It's a fact.

TAMAM: Looks are a commodity, an asset, a possession
I happen to possess.
It's why my grandmother said

CHORUS: (ARCHITECT & DELILAH) no,

TAMAM:
when my sister's brother in law asked for my hand.
The family that was good enough
for my plain sister wasn't good enough for me.
I'm a pretty woman.
It's not a boast.

CHORUS: (ARCHITECT & DELILAH) It's a fact.

TAMAM: And I smiled my best smile
When the soldiers opened the gate for me.

CHORUS: (ARCHITECT & DELILAH)
Weighed down with baskets of food,

TAMAM: I brought extra,
hoping to create the illusion

that that dirty jail was one place
where there was enough and extra for all
the guards to eat twice.
Otherwise, my brother would get none.
unless there was enough and extra.

CHORUS: (ARCHITECT & DELILAH)
They thanked me

TAMAM: for the food.
And they raped me in front of him,
forcing my brother's eyes open so he had to watch.
They wanted to know something

AIESHA: that he apparently preferred not to tell them.

TAMAM: They skewered the support for their argument
into my flesh.
The crusaders believed rape would enrage our men.

CHORUS: (ARCHITECT, DELILAH &TAMAM)
Enraging a man is the first step on the stairway

TAMAM: that gets him to a place
where he becomes impotent,
helpless.
Say what you want about Arab men and women
and how we love one another,
There is one thing that's for certain.
There are real repercussions for hurting a woman in my
society.

CHORUS: (AIESHA, ARCHITECT, DELILAH & TAMAM)
There are repercussions.

TAMAM: When the first hand was laid upon me, we
both screamed.
The evolutionary function of a scream is a cry for help,
they tied down the only one who could
so I silenced myself.
That was the only way to tell my brother
I didn't want him to tell.

I flinched when I had to,
but I kept my breathing regular.
My brother tried to look every other way,
but realized I needed him,
to look me in the eyes
(*Pause*) and understand.
They thought making us face one another
in our misery would break us.
But we were used to misery.
It's like anything else.

AIESHA: You can build up a tolerance for it.

TAMAM:
Someone else told them what they wanted to know,
so they released my brother two weeks later.

CHORUS: (ARCHITECT & DELILAH) That's when he
joined a rebel group organized in a prison.

TAMAM:
The group sent each man alone at the same time
to a different part of the crowded Crusader marketplace,

CHORUS: (ARCHITECT, DELILAH & TAMAM)
Each with a knife and a double-ball battle mace,
killing as many as they could till—

DELILAH: Is that an arm?

ARCHITECT: A hand. Who does it belong to?

TAMAM: Full of men, women, children

DELILAH: No, it's a spine. Look at the ridges.

ARCHITECT: Who does it belong to?

TAMAM: Pilgrims—not warriors.
People—not parts of flesh strewn everywhere,
until my brother and the others got there.
My brother's parts mixed in

with the people he believed could not stand him.
Because he believed they could not stand him.

CHORUS: (ARCHITECT & DELILAH)
Who does it belong to?

TAMAM: I was not allowed to bury what I gathered
What I believed to be

CHORUS: (ARCHITECT, DELILAH & TAMAM) Parts of him,

TAMAM: The Crusader mourners pulled
the one hand

CHORUS: (ARCHITECT, DELILAH & TAMAM)
that I was sure was his

TAMAM: out of mine.
They smeared it and his head with pig fat,
as they did to desecrate the bodies of our soldiers.
They hung my brother's head and hand with them
on pikes above the city walls
The head I barely recognized,
but I wanted to bury his hand

CHORUS: (ARCHITECT & DELILAH)
To show who it belonged to.

TAMAM: The day he did it,
he told me over breakfast—
Oppression

AIESHA: is like a coin maker.

TAMAM: You put in human beings,
press the right buttons and
watch them
get squeezed, shrunk, flattened
till they take the slim shape of a two-faced coin

TAMAM: One side is a martyr,

AIESHA: the other a traitor.

TAMAM: All the possibilities of a life get reduced to
those paltry two.
The coin is tossed in the air
it spins once for circumstance,
twice for luck,
and a third time for predilection
before it lands flat.
The face that points down

CHORUS: (ARCHITECT & DELILAH) towards hell

TAMAM: determines not only who you are,

CHORUS: (ARCHITECT & DELILAH)
but how you will become that way.

TAMAM: What he was really saying was

TAMAM & AIESHA: good-bye.

TAMAM: Had I known, I would have said something
more than—
"Brother, it's interesting you think oppression
makes us turn into a form of money, a currency.

CHORUS: (ARCHITECT & DELILAH) How odd."

TAMAM:
Listen, I don't agree with killing innocent people
under any circumstances,

CHORUS: (ARCHITECT, DELILAH & TAMAM) Ever.

TAMAM: I am the kind of human being
who refuses to get addicted to

CHORUS: (ARCHITECT, DELILAH & TAMAM)
the intoxication of hate.

TAMAM: In my opinion,

CHORUS: (ARCHITECT, DELILAH & TAMAM)
that's the only kind of human being there is.

TAMAM:
In other words, no one is going to reduce me to a coin.
There are absolutes,
it's wrong to kill, period.

ARCHITECT: Hands! Movement!

AIESHA: *(Overlapping with* ARCHITECT's *line)* Not always.

TAMAM:
I should have known what my brother was bound to do,
I could have stopped him.
I said every time he went out to fight.
"Don't go.
We'll achieve peace by peaceful means.

CHORUS: (ARCHITECT & DELILAH) Don't be a pawn.

TAMAM: Let others risk their lives.
With all their weapons,
these foreigners can never truly win.

CHORUS: (ARCHITECT & DELILAH) They can't kill us all.

TAMAM: I'd always say

CHORUS: (ARCHITECT, DELILAH & TAMAM) Don't go.

TAMAM: But I didn't say
"You are the most precious thing in the world to me.
The fact that you exist makes the earth spin on its axis,
it's rolling for joy because you are here.
The sun shows up to see you,
and the moon chases the sun off to be in your sky
and none of them love you like I do, brother.

CHORUS: (ARCHITECT & DELILAH) Not even close.

TAMAM: If you think this is a gift for me,
the box will be empty, brother.

CHORUS: (ARCHITECT & DELILAH)
How can it not be?

TAMAM: Everything will be empty, if you're not here.
I will not forgive you if you leave me.
I will not be comforted.
I will not be."
Instead I said

CHORUS: (AIESHA, ARCHITECT & DELILAH) don't go

TAMAM: And I didn't say it loud.
Brother, they burned down our entire village
because you killed those people.
What you did wasn't about my honor.
It was about yours.
It is braver,

CHORUS: (ARCHITECT, DELILAH & TAMAM) harder,

TAMAM: to live in a place
where no one wants us to live
than to die and leave me like that.
I didn't want revenge.
I wanted my brother alive.
My name is Tamam.
It means enough.
Go tell my brother I'm here.

(Pause)

AIESHA: Boo hoo. Boo hoo. Boo fucking hoo.
What a horrible life you had on earth.
Get over it.

TAMAM:
I'm over it. Now go on and ask about my brother.

AIESHA: And you actually think he's going to want to
see you, Miss Enough?

TAMAM: Yes.

AIESHA: So you can insult him? Was your brother the
type that took well to having his choices questioned?

TAMAM: Why does it matter?

AIESHA: If you don't think it matters, go right in.
I'm sure you'll be fine.
It's only a room full of, um, I don't know, let me
see...martyrs!
So I suggest that you don't go in telling some story that
dares to question the value of self-sacrifice.

TAMAM: So what do I say instead?

AIESHA: You could start by acknowledging your story
is not unique. You were raped and lost a brother to war.
That happened to millions of women throughout
history. In fact, the Crusades were nothing compared to
the Palestinian and Israeli wars I lived through.

TAMAM: The solution to that one was so easy, Aiesha.

DELILAH: Yes, Aiesha.
The Palestinian-Israeli problem was solved ages ago.

TAMAM, DELILAH, ARCHITECT: One state called
the United States of Israel and Palestine.

DELILAH: Pal-rael for short.

TAMAM: The posters for travel agents everywhere boast
first-class packages to Pal-rael that say

TAMAM, DELILAH, ARCHITECT: "Come to Pal-rael.
It's safe
because the Palestinians and Israelis are now real pals.

TAMAM: Come see the Pal-rael museum of the centuries
of war.

ARCHITECT: It was built so both peoples of Pal-rael
could be reminded of their dark past.

DELILAH: You go to remember that all the killing and
struggling on both sides was in vain.

AIESHA: My struggle—

TAMAM: in vain...

AIESHA: The death of our loved ones—

ARCHITECT: ourselves—

TAMAM: in vain.

AIESHA: It's true. I can't believe it.

DELILAH: And it happened in your lifetime. Or rather would have if you had stuck around a bit longer. Now, there are other hot spots in the world.

TAMAM: Flash points of pain.

ARCHITECT: The Swedes have now gone buck wild,

TAMAM: are angry that the Maltese continue to make fun of the fact that they have no eyelashes.

DELILAH: The Swedes insist we have eyelashes, but they are blond and therefore invisible to the naked eye.

CHORUS: (ARCHITECT, DELILAH & TAMAM) War ensued.

TAMAM: It may sound kind of amusing.
And you can laugh and laugh,

ARCHITECT & TAMAM: Unless...

DELILAH: You're a Maltese mother who watched a soldier slit her son's throat

CHORUS: (ARCHITECT, DELILAH & TAMAM)
From ear to ear

DELILAH: or a Swedish sister whose brother walked out one day

CHORUS: (ARCHITECT, DELILAH & TAMAM)
and never came back.

TAMAM:
Unless you lost someone who was everything to you.
I've been in heaven for over hundreds of years.
I have seen every person, even the guards who raped me,

who apologized profusely.
And, what they believed,
what they feared even as they raped me,
would eventually happen did happen.
I was the first person to greet them in the after-life
and I was allowed to cut off their genitals.
But I chose not to and said I'll be back to do it later,
because I didn't want to hurt them once and be done
with it.
I wanted them to fear me forever.

CHORUS: (ARCHITECT & DELILAH)
Wouldn't you rather let it go?
It would be a sign that you have grown, healed.

TAMAM: Hell no.
Those soldiers killed more than my brother did, I'm
sure.
And yet they are still here, roaming free.
I have seen everyone,
except the dearest person in the world to me.
So, if the war I suffered under is truly over,
why is my brother in that room?
Why is he not with me?

ARCHITECT: Tell her. (Pause) Tell her.

AIESHA: Maybe I will, maybe I won't.

ARCHITECT: Tell her and tell me why did I have to die
like that?

AIESHA: I don't know how or why you died.
I'm getting tired of you, you little idiot.

ARCHITECT: I may be inarticulate.
Have always been.
It's not that I'm not thinking clear thoughts,
I'm thinking too many of them.
Hands, movement, change!
(To AIESHA) Murderer!

TAMAM: *(To* ARCHITECT*)* That's enough, honey.

ARCHITECT: *(To* AIESHA*)* I know your face.

AIESHA: Do you have something to say?

ARCHITECT: Yes!
But can I say it?
Why must I speak in words when I think in images?
Hands! Movement! Change!
I'm an architect of unseen structures
and buildings that will never be built.
I am the mother of children who will never be born,

CHORUS: *(*DELILAH *&* TAMAM*)*
the lover of men who will remain unloved.

ARCHITECT: No, men who are loved beyond compare,
but will never know it.

CHORUS: *(*DELILAH *&* TAMAM*)*
Or how their lives would be changed if they did.

ARCHITECT: Right.
It was all the Half-Breed's fault.
Meeting that son of a bitch led to my murder.
This, like so many things, all started with a

CHORUS: *(*DELILAH *&* TAMAM*)* job interview.

ARCHITECT: He had an Arab last name.

CHORUS: *(*DELILAH *&* TAMAM*)* Half-Breed.

ARCHITECT: I was always falling for the Half-Breeds.
I can even see him in front of me now.
(Addresses DELILAH *as if she is the Half-Breed)*
I walked into your office, Half-Breed
applying for an assistantship.
I read all about you in *Architectural Digest.*
Your daddy's a Christian Palestinian,
like my parents are.
But your mama's

CHORUS: (DELILAH & TAMAM)
white.

ARCHITECT:
You're a son of bitch with that side way smile,
that you flash when I walk in.
You were discussing Gehry's new museum with your
minions.
Nice as hell you were,
asking me what I thought of the new museum,
as if my opinion mattered
as if I mattered...
You were polite,

CHORUS: (DELILAH & TAMAM) too polite,

ARCHITECT: to someone applying to be an assistant.
And everyone in the room knew it.
Sidelong glances, and smirks from your minions
He's at it again, their eyes say.

CHORUS: (DELILAH) I'm at it again

ARCHITECT: Your eyes say.
I'm glad you asked me.
Architecture is the only thing I can be articulate about.
"I think Gehry's work is over..."
Your eyes never leave mine as
your head cocks to one side.
"...indulgent."
I meant to say rated!

CHORUS: (DELILAH)
"Why do you say that?"

ARCHITECT: The answer is you make me nervous.
You make me say over-indulgent when I meant
overrated.
If you didn't, I'd still be articulate
about the one thing I can be articulate about.
If that flash in your eyes wasn't signaling,

CHORUS: (DELILAH) We don't have to be here.
You and I.
We could, in fact, be somewhere else.

ARCHITECT: while your lips are asking me...

CHORUS: (DELILAH & ARCHITECT) "How would you

CHORUS: (DELILAH) do it?"

ARCHITECT:
If I was articulate, I'd say, "hire me and find out."
But I'm not,
so I pull out the drawing I happen to have,
the draft I made on the train coming over,
You see I do little projects.
I take

CHORUS: (DELILAH & TAMAM)
the requirements and dimensions

ARCHITECT: that clients give to far too many overrated
white men like Gehry to make a museum.
and make my own drawings
of how I would do it
if some gave me

CHORUS: (DELILAH & TAMAM) a chance.

ARCHITECT:
And on the ride over to meet you, Half-Breed.
I happened to be working on
my version of the museum
you and your minions—in your jealousy—were
denigrating.

CHORUS: (DELILAH & TAMAM) An exercise

ARCHITECT: you might say, if you didn't know
how desperate I get on trains.
I have what I call....

CHORUS: (ARCHITECT, DELILAH & TAMAM)
Day-mares.

ARCHITECT: Every time I step on a train, I think
what if

CHORUS: (DELILAH & TAMAM) what if

ARCHITECT: what if
I'll always be stuck in this place
where no one is allowed to talk to one another
while trying to get to a place where people hopefully
do?
So I take out a piece of paper and sketch
and scrap and sketch again.
I never show the work I do on trains to anyone,
why I gave it to you,

CHORUS: (DELILAH & TAMAM) God only knows.

ARCHITECT: You appraise it, the way you appraise
everything in your path,
including me in my well-tailored suit.
If you were to touch me, Half-Breed,
I would pull out handfuls of your hair,

CHORUS: (DELILAH & TAMAM) not against,

ARCHITECT: but towards me!
I can already feel how your hands
will work,

CHORUS: (DELILAH & TAMAM) Sculpt,

ARCHITECT: Grasp
fingers full of my flesh
like clay in your arms.
I'll want to tell you
"It's like you're shaping me!

CHORUS: (DELILAH & TAMAM) You're shaping me!"

ARCHITECT: But I'm not articulate, so I'll probably just—

CHORUS: (ARCHITECT, DELILAH & TAMAM) pant.

ARCHITECT: I'm thinking all this while you are
still staring at my draft, my exercise.

CHORUS: (DELILAH & TAMAM) Buying time.

ARCHITECT: Though there might be none for sale.
I would marry you in a heartbeat.
Our children will have an Arab last name
and I will raise them in the culture you do not know
and you will not understand why I'm still a virgin at
thirty,

CHORUS: (DELILAH)
My father's tongue is not my mother tongue.

ARCHITECT:
I don't speak hardly a lick of the Arabic language either,
but I can make out the morsels that count.
You will not know
that the only thing you've got going for you is
you have a chance of understanding
the two languages I was born to learn and love.

CHORUS: (DELILAH & TAMAM) Arabic and architecture.

ARCHITECT: I live with my parents,
always have,

CHORUS: (DELILAH & TAMAM) always will

ARCHITECT: till a man takes me from my father's house.
Half-Breed, can I explain why
if you want me
it's important your people come to my home on the day
we marry,
so that you know I do not come from nothing?
The bejeweled old peacock women of my clan
who you pray I won't look like in forty years,

CHORUS: (DELILAH & TAMAM) though I'd be proud
to have half the strength of the least of them.

ARCHITECT:
will come to my house to make their presence known.
to trill and clap, but really to show you
that if you hurt me...
these bejeweled old women
can fly up like birds and peck out your eyes.
What they're saying by showing up to my house early,
witnessing your people escort me from it
is
we are watching...

CHORUS: (DELILAH & TAMAM)
If you fuck with her, you fuck with us.

ARCHITECT: But you won't know our customs.
Half-Breed!
Your mother wasn't Arab.

CHORUS: (DELILAH & TAMAM)
Mothers teach their children early
the customs and morals and superstitions that stick.

ARCHITECT: My mother always told me

CHORUS: (TAMAM)
Marry an Arab man.
They have a little sense of decency.

ARCHITECT:
She means they don't often abandon their families.
My mother thinks if a man doesn't leave you,
that means he loves you,

CHORUS: (DELILAH & TAMAM)
in the way men know how to love.

ARCHITECT:
I would marry you in a heartbeat, Half-Breed.
Give you my hand,
and hope you learned how to be a man from your
father.

CHORUS: (ARCHITECT, DELILAH & TAMAM)
I have designs on your heart.

ARCHITECT: But I don't know how to execute them.
Why can't love be as easy as architecture?
Half-Breed, you like me and I like you.
I wish I could just show you
a draft of the nest I would build for us,
with a room for each child I want to have.
A house with no master bedroom.
A house with no masters.
The only thing I'll have to say is...

CHORUS: (DELILAH & TAMAM)
Do you like this house? Just say yes or no.

ARCHITECT:
And you will understand my question to mean

CHORUS: (DELILAH & TAMAM)
Do you want to live here with me forever? Yes or no.

ARCHITECT: Put the plans in motion or no.
Lay down the first twig of our nest in the nook of a tree
that won't be felled or

CHORUS: (DELILAH & TAMAM) no!

ARCHITECT:
All this I think of as I look at you looking at my draft.
I stare at you, Half-Breed.
And from the time it takes you to lift your eyes
from the page to mine,
this is what I think on...
Will our children have your doe eyes or my black ones?
I think of how I will stop making drafts on subways,
because I want our youngest son to recite for me his A
B Cs and one, two, threes.

Our daughter is so arrogant already.
Just like me.

Arrogance is confidence that is snuffed out,
resuscitated,
and is never quite the same again.

CHORUS: (DELILAH & TAMAM) Weaker and meaner.

ARCHITECT: Unrecognizable.
Arrogance is what happens to a confident girl
when the whole world, or even just her mother,
tells her that she's nothing and she finds out
she's really something.

CHORUS: (DELILAH & TAMAM) Really something.

ARCHITECT: I'll tell myself
it's no big tragedy that I rarely sketch anymore.
It's my choice, really.
You tell me

CHORUS: (DELILAH) Get a nanny, if you want to...

ARCHITECT: As if what I want ever has anything to do
with what I get.
Occasionally a female architect like Zaha Hadid
succeeds,
but its mostly men like Gehry and you, Half-Breed
husband,
who get to design museums.
I wipe asses because they are the most beautiful perfect
little asses imaginable,
and no one would wipe them the way I do!

I content myself with helping you with your work,
showing you where you falter, and you falter often
enough.

CHORUS: (DELILAH & TAMAM)
It's not sound. It's not sound,
and it's being built on a fault line.

ARCHITECT:
Was your head up your ass when you designed this?!

CHORUS: (DELILAH & TAMAM)
Or was it up someone else's?

ARCHITECT: But I can't say that.
I'll have to be vague and suggest
A reinforcement or two.
I have to be careful not to bruise your ego.

CHORUS: (DELILAH & TAMAM)
Because we all know what happens when that happens.

ARCHITECT: You have your women.
But you never leave me.
That's cold comfort and I'm in the winter of my life.

CHORUS: (DELILAH & TAMAM)
But it's comfort just the same.

ARCHITECT: I'm like cement
You pour me, I fit the mold of a wife, and stay there

AIESHA: until you crack.

ARCHITECT: I'll smile softly when I overhear them
saying about me—

CHORUS: (DELILAH & TAMAM)
"She's an architect in her own right too."

ARCHITECT: In my own right, they will say,
which always makes me think,
my relationship with you makes
what is my right somehow in question.

CHORUS: (DELILAH & TAMAM) Why must one speak in
words when she thinks in images?

ARCHITECT: You lift your head from my page,
Your eyes finally meet mine.
You smile.

CHORUS: (DELILAH & ARCHITECT)
I can make you fall in love with me

ARCHITECT: but never feel secure in that love.
I know that, if I encourage you, twenty years

CHORUS: (DELILAH & TAMAM) from now

ARCHITECT: I will be sitting on the toilet
in a hotel ballroom
on a night you get some award
for a project I did at least half the work on.
Two girls will enter,
about the age I am now,
and one will be bragging in a sing-song voice to the
other...

CHORUS: (TAMAM)
"I did it with him again on Sunday. In his office."

ARCHITECT:
She won't have to say his name for me to know,
which him she's singing about.
My Half-Breed husband!
My mind will flip back to Sunday afternoon
when you said...

CHORUS: (DELILAH) "I'm going to the office to finish up
the project I'm working on."

ARCHITECT: Sunday is my day.
You take the children and I do my work
But I don't insist, you usually give me my Sundays.
I don't complain because the one time I tried.
You told me

CHORUS: (DELILAH) Give me a fucking break.
Whose work pays the bills?

CHORUS: (DELILAH & TAMAM) Who pays the bills?

ARCHITECT: I don't cost much to feed nowadays.
You're a big fat motherfucker now.
I weigh much less than the day you married me
because I have to stay

thin,
gaunt,
hollow.

CHORUS: (DELILAH & TAMAM) Take up less space!
Take up less space!

ARCHITECT:
I stay thin so no one can say that I'm not trying

CHORUS: (DELILAH & TAMAM) to be in control!

AIESHA: Stay in control.

CHORUS: (DELILAH) Who pays the bills?

ARCHITECT: If I was articulate, I would say,
"I do!
I organize every aspect your life
so you can do your life's work."
But I know that's not what you mean.
Most people ask for one day of rest, I beg for one day of
work
and you

CHORUS: (ARCHITECT, DELILAH & TAMAM)
can't give it to me!

ARCHITECT: But I don't complain on that Sunday
and you go to work on

CHORUS: (DELILAH & TAMAM) your project.

ARCHITECT: And that was the day I slapped my
daughter hard
across the face.

(TAMAM and DELILAH clap once at the same time.)

ARCHITECT: She gave me a look that said—

CHORUS: (TAMAM) I did not deserve that.

ARCHITECT: I will not forget that you did that to me and
I didn't deserve it.

CHORUS: (TAMAM) Not even the day you die.

ARCHITECT: That was last Sunday.
I will leave the bathroom and join you at the table of

CHORUS: (DELILAH & TAMAM) honor.

ARCHITECT: You smile when our eyes meet from across
the banquet hall.
I think about what you told me on the way over here

CHORUS: (DELILAH) My wife's still a pretty woman.
It's not a boast, it's a fact.

ARCHITECT: I sit next to you, Half-Breed husband.
You can tell I'm upset.
Everyone can tell.

CHORUS: (DELILAH & TAMAM) You cock...

ARCHITECT: ...your head to the side,
questioning at first.

CHORUS: (DELILAH) "What's wrong, honey?"

ARCHITECT: Then you see the look in my eyes, you
don't ask again.
You let it go.
I'll tell myself to just lighten up and get over it.
There are people dying in Palestine.

AIESHA: There are people dying in Palestine.

ARCHITECT:
And I very easily could have been one of them.
In marriage, there are worse crimes than infidelity.

CHORUS: (DELILAH & TAMAM) He still falls asleep
stroking your cheek.

ARCHITECT: I now even think it's endearing that he is
jealous of my work,
that he needs all my time and attention when he's home.

CHORUS: (DELILAH & TAMAM) Like a child.

ARCHITECT:
Soon enough, I'll be staring at you in your coffin.
Our three-quarter breed children will be crying...

CHORUS: (DELILAH & TAMAM) Baba!

ARCHITECT: Because I made our three-quarter breed
children use the Arabic words for family members.
Always.
They'll be crying...

CHORUS: (DELILAH)
"Excuse me, would you like to go somewhere and
(Pause) have coffee?"

ARCHITECT:
Your question interrupts my thoughts, Half-Breed.
It startles me.
I didn't notice you were done looking at my exercise
and holding it out for me to take back.
I think to myself—
Why are you talking to me?
Can't you see I'm in the middle of envisioning our
future together?
I realize that I've done it again.
In my mind, I planned a whole life—

CHORUS: (DELILAH & TAMAM) Birth,
death,
remembrance.

ARCHITECT: with a guy
before he even asks me out.
Why does my mind flip a lifetime ahead?
We might go out and not hit it off.
I mean, for God's sake, you could be gay
I could be reading all the signs wrong.
It has happened to me before.
You've just asked me for coffee.
Why am I imagining your funereal
with our children standing before you screaming

CHORUS: (DELILAH & TAMAM) Baba!

ARCHITECT: Why am I sure
as I stare into your eyes, trying to decide if I want to
have coffee with you,
that, if I say yes, one day
I'll be staring at your corpse in your coffin,
thinking a thousand thoughts,
not the least of which will be—
There lies your body. Your flesh,
that you valued more than my heart, my love, our
family, and my life.
Let. it. rot!

CHORUS: (DELILAH)
"I said, would you like to have coffee with me?"

ARCHITECT: "No! No! No!"

CHORUS: (DELILAH) "Tea?"

ARCHITECT: And I decline that too, saying I have to go
right back home.
We worked together for a summer and he's always

CHORUS: (DELILAH & TAMAM)
polite

ARCHITECT:
but he never offers to quench thirsts with me again.
(Pause) Then, I was murdered.
And, as a result, I died.
Do you understand now?
Do you see now that she's lying?

DELILAH & TAMAM: No.

AIESHA: Ha! I knew you were a half-wit.

ARCHITECT: (To DELILAH and TAMAM)
She's going to try to distract you
She's going to keep you here.

AIESHA: All right you two. If you want my help—

ARCHITECT: Stop pretending you're going to
eventually lead them through that door.

AIESHA:
Stop pretending you know something about me.

ARCHITECT: *(To* AIESHA*)*
I'm getting to how I know who you are.

TAMAM: What does this encounter with a Half-Breed
have to do with this woman?

DELILAH: Why shouldn't we trust her?
Can you tell us in a way we will understand?

ARCHITECT: Yes.
My contract with the Half-Breed's company was not
renewed.
I was told I was not a team player.

CHORUS: (DELILAH & TAMAM) Five years passed.

ARCHITECT: I stayed friends with his assistant so I could
keep tabs on the Half-Breed.
On my thirty-fifth birthday, I called him.
You see I had promised myself
If I'm not married by thirty-five,
I would stop being precious and just have sex
with a man I wanted to love me,
whether or not he did.

CHORUS: (DELILAH & TAMAM) Why thirty-five?

ARCHITECT: Because it's no longer cute
that you're a virgin at thirty-five.

CHORUS: (DELILAH & TAMAM) I called him.

ARCHITECT: I told him my name. He said—

CHORUS: (DELILAH) "You're the girl who worked as an
assistant that summer,
who walked into the interview

with a plan for a museum,
right?"

ARCHITECT:
"I want to come see you. I want to come stay with you."

CHORUS: (DELILAH) "Get on the next flight."

ARCHITECT: And I do so!
I've got two fantasies, day-mares, about flying.

CHORUS: (DELILAH & TAMAM)
First fantasy I have as I'm going through
the security check

ARCHITECT: on my way to see the Half-Breed.
It's totally stupid, okay?
But you've got to understand,
I grew up watching American movies
and so I've got this fantasy.
That I'll be on a flight, okay, and it'll be hijacked by my
people, Arabs.

CHORUS: (AIESHA) Sounds stupid.

ARCHITECT: I already admitted it was.
But in my fantasy
I'll hear the shouts first in my mother's tongue
that my mother never bothered to teach me to speak.
And I understand what they're saying:
I realize the power of language—
that being able to listen and understand is a different
kind of articulacy
and one I possess.
Like how I can't speak Arabic, but I can comprehend

CHORUS: (DELILAH & TAMAM)
and know what's going on before everyone else does.

ARCHITECT: In my fantasy,
all the men are fit and handsome.
They don't intend to kill anybody.

CHORUS: (DELILAH & TAMAM)
They've lived lives that would break the hardest of men.

ARCHITECT: They only want to be heard.
Dramatic music will play.
I will stand up,
perfectly manicured and dressed to the meet the press,
I will say in perfect Arabic to the men.

CHORUS: (AIESHA) But you can't speak Arabic?

ARCHITECT: This is my fantasy, goddamn it!
And in it, I speak perfect Arabic.
I will stand up
and talk those men out of their plans.
I will tell them

CHORUS: (ARCHITECT, DELILAH & TAMAM)
So what if terror helped bring down apartheid in South
Africa?

CHORUS: (TAMAM)
So what if the Black Panther Movement got civil rights
workers moving
just a little bit quicker?

CHORUS: (DELILAH)
So what if the American government supports corrupt
leaders
in our countries and then kills
hundreds of thousands of Arabs
when those leaders don't do

CHORUS: (ARCHITECT, DELILAH & TAMAM)
what they say
when they say it?

ARCHITECT: All that still doesn't make it right to kill.
I would say to them—
You're hijacking this plane full of people who are
ignorant,
who are looking at you and saying—

CHORUS: *(*DELILAH *&* TAMAM*)*
What kind of people could do such violent, cruel things?

ARCHITECT: They don't know that it's the kind of people
The American government has been doing
just as violent, cruel things to
in its people's name for generations.
Maybe they don't care.
But they're not worth killing yourself over.
They call us terrorists.

CHORUS: *(*DELILAH *&* TAMAM*)* They are wrong!

ARCHITECT: We're too good a people to do such harm.
I would tell them
I am a Palestinian.
I lived like an Arab in America.
I even only dated my own kind,
because I wanted someone who understood
the first words my family taught me to mean love.

CHORUS: *(*DELILAH *&* TAMAM*)*
Ha-beeb-tea.

ARCHITECT: Even after I realized,
just because a man knows the right words
doesn't mean that he will say them
and, even if he says them,
it doesn't mean that he means them.
I will tell those men.

CHORUS: *(*ARCHITECT, DELILAH *&* TAMAM*)*
I was never ashamed of who I was.

ARCHITECT: I knew I had to synthesize all the
signals about who I was
in a way
that made me not want to be anything else.
I knew if I was not proud to be a Palestinian,
I could not live a life with dignity.

I knew if I did not love my people, no one would.
I would tell them all this

CHORUS: (DELILAH & TAMAM) and more!

ARCHITECT: And, when I tell them about my life, it will
seem like it has
a relevance,
a grace,
an arc,

CHORUS: (DELILAH & TAMAM) a worth

ARCHITECT: that I didn't realize it had before.
They will realize it too.
I would no longer resent being a bridge between two
cultures,
or ask myself...

CHORUS: (ARCHITECT, DELILAH & TAMAM)
What does a bridge ever do except get stepped on?

ARCHITECT:
Because I was so articulate in my perfect Arabic,
the plane would touch down safely.
All the Americans in the plane would listen to the
grievances of the
men who were willing to kill and die to be heard.

CHORUS: (DELILAH & TAMAM)
They would be moved by stories of those they feared.

ARCHITECT: In fact, they'll refuse to get off of the plane,
until Palestinians are allowed the right to
self-determination,
Iraqis are not killed so their oil can be stolen,
The people on the plane don't buy the crap the
American government
tries to sell us about trying to secure human rights...

CHORUS: (DELILAH & TAMAM)
having the gall to use human rights

ARCHITECT: as an excuse to bomb those human beings
while being allies,

CHORUS: (AIESHA) bedfellows,

ARCHITECT: with the oppressive Saudi
royal-pain-in-the-ass regime because

CHORUS: (AIESHA) they give up their juice.

ARCHITECT: When all those conditions are met,
everyone on the plane leaves safely.
There will be a movie made about me.
I would end up on Oprah, telling my story.
I will be articulate.
One of the audience members will tell me,

CHORUS: (DELILAH)
Julia Roberts does a great job playing you in the movie.
I'm glad she acknowledged you at the Academy
Awards.
But I've got to say...

CHORUS: (DELILAH & TAMAM)
We the P T A board members of Lansing, Michigan
think you're even prettier than Julia is.

ARCHITECT: Then Oprah will say

CHORUS: (TAMAM)
More importantly, she's also a brilliant architect.

ARCHITECT:
But she won't have to say "in her own right."
Before the first commercial break,
it'll be clear that Oprah and I are now best friends.
I'll let her announce that I've been commissioned to
design
the new United Nations building
since the old one obviously wasn't engineered to work
right.
And, in my fantasy, the love of my life

who may or may not be the Half-Breed,
because maybe when my people are no longer under
siege,

CHORUS: (DELILAH & TAMAM) no longer a dying breed,

ARCHITECT: I won't feel I owe it to my people to mate
with my own kind.
I'll be free

CHORUS: (DELILAH & TAMAM)
in the most important way it is to be free.

ARCHITECT: I'll be free to love who I love.
And whoever that man who I love is,
he will be sitting in the audience.
Our eyes will connect for the slightest second
We'll remember

CHORUS: (TAMAM)
We don't have to stay here much longer.
You and I, we will soon go somewhere else.

ARCHITECT: I'll feel a shot of warmth in me,
like a dying fire that with one breath he can keep aglow.

I will be a hero like Doctor King or Gandhi,
but no one shoots me.
Did everyone hear that? No one shoots me.
That's not part of the fantasy I have as I go through the
security check on my way to lose my virginity to the
Half-Breed.
I don't want to die that way.

AIESHA: Does anybody want to die that way?

ARCHITECT:
No. And no one wants to die the way I did, either.
Hands, change!

(AIESHA bursts into laughter.)

ARCHITECT: Small! Change hands! Movement.

AIESHA: She speaks gibberish.

TAMAM: *(To* ARCHITECT*)* We're still listening.

DELILAH: You're going through the security check—

ARCHITECT: Right, and I think to myself—
what a stupid fantasy that is.
I've clearly been watching too many American movies.
I will refuse to watch the one on the flight.
I think that to myself as I give the girl at the counter my ticket.
I'm afraid to fly. So much of my life is lived in the space between

CHORUS: *(*DELILAH *&* TAMAM*)* fear and desire.

ARCHITECT: I know if my plane were to go down,
there is one thing I would truly regret.
And that leads me to the next fantasy I have while settling in my seat
on the plane
which will take me to the place
where I will lose my virginity to the Half-Breed.
I look for the straps of my seatbelt.
Knowing I'm a beast,

CHORUS: *(*DELILAH *&* TAMAM*)* animal,

ARCHITECT: beast, but to have been a beast with only one back all my life.
To die a virgin!

CHORUS: *(*AIESHA*)* What a tragedy that would be.

ARCHITECT: Tell me about it. So my fantasy as I strap my seatbelt on—

CHORUS: *(*DELILAH *&* TAMAM*)* Click.

ARCHITECT: is that if I somehow figure out that
this plane is going to crash.
And I realize I'm going to die a virgin.
I'd stomp up to the

CHORUS: *(DELILAH & TAMAM)* cock

ARCHITECT:
pit. And who says language isn't everything?
And once I get to the

CHORUS: *(DELILAH & TAMAM)* cock

ARCHITECT: pit, I'd get on that loudspeaker and say—
"Unfasten your seatbelts.

CHORUS: *(ARCHITECT, DELILAH & TAMAM)*
Motherfuckers!

ARCHITECT: If this plane is going down,
someone is going down on me!"

CHORUS: *(DELILAH & TAMAM)*
But one rarely has the guts to act out fantasies.

ARCHITECT: So even if the plane went down
by accident

CHORUS: *(DELILAH & TAMAM)*
technical failure instead of the emotional kind.

ARCHITECT: I probably would not go up to the

CHORUS: *(DELILAH & TAMAM)* cock

ARCHITECT: pit and say that.
I would have sat in my seat like I

CHORUS: *(DELILAH & TAMAM)* sat in the seat of disbelief.

ARCHITECT: when I actually did hear those men
shouting in my mother's tongue
and it wasn't a fantasy.
It was real.
It was my life.
It was awful.
I knew what they were saying and I knew what they
were doing

CHORUS: *(DELILAH & TAMAM)* before anyone else did.

ARCHITECT: One of them passed by my row and I
thought to myself...
as if I was an American with ancestors on the
Mayflower
and had no understanding of America's history
in the Middle East.
I thought to myself—

CHORUS: (DELILAH & TAMAM)
What kind of person could do such a thing?

ARCHITECT: The one who ran past me was chubby

CHORUS: (DELILAH & TAMAM) like my brothers.

ARCHITECT: Stupid me, always thinking—

CHORUS: (DELILAH & TAMAM)
inappropriate thoughts.

ARCHITECT: Thoughts that make me thank heaven I am
so inarticulate.
As the man tied up a stewardess....
I was thinking I like chubby men.
I don't trust men if they're too thin.
I don't trust men
if they aren't susceptible
to the least pernicious of appetites.

CHORUS: (DELILAH & TAMAM)
I think you just don't trust men.

ARCHITECT: He passed my row and our eyes met.
Perhaps because I was the only one looking up,
not crying.
He froze.
The way Arabs outside the Arab world do
when they recognize that someone here

CHORUS: (DELILAH & TAMAM) is one of my kind.

ARCHITECT: He waited for me to speak
and when I couldn't,

he went on his way without a backward glance.
From the look in his eyes,
I lost all hope that any of us would live.
I took out my sketch book
and sketched for the first time

CHORUS: (DELILAH & TAMAM) without fear.

ARCHITECT: I took out my sketch book,
did my work

CHORUS: (DELILAH & TAMAM)
and saw that it was good.

ARCHITECT: I'm here to find that man who passed me
and knew I was an Arab.
He's in that room in front of us.
I know it.
Just like I know that I could have stopped him
before he did what he did
if I had the right words

CHORUS: (DELILAH & TAMAM) Don't blame yourself.

ARCHITECT: It's not about blame. What's the point of
being articulate when no one
can hear anything they aren't ready to hear?

CHORUS: (DELILAH & TAMAM) It's not about blame.

ARCHITECT:
It's about knowing that there are always words—

CHORUS: (DELILAH & TAMAM)
Words that work like spells

ARCHITECT: something you can say
that will stop someone from doing something

CHORUS: (DELILAH & TAMAM) awful.

ARCHITECT: The man who killed me is the only one
who can tell me

CHORUS: (DELILAH & TAMAM) what those words are.

ARCHITECT: I'm here to ask him.
If anyone gives me trouble while I'm trying to get in,
I will tell them,
I died a virgin, but that was just bad luck.
While I was alive, I did the hardest thing imaginable,
more wonderful than a million buildings that will one
day crumble.
I am a woman who was born with a good heart
and I designed and executed my life in a way that made
sure
that's how I would stay.

The image I had in my mind
during the last moment I was alive
was of your face.
I died thinking I hope people won't see me where I saw
you.

AIESHA: You've never seen me.

ARCHITECT: The night before I boarded that plane and
died on it,
I had insomnia.
It was my last night as a virgin.
Or so I believed.
I couldn't sleep.
I was on my computer
using search engines to seek
out the sites of hate that cry—

CHORUS: (DELILAH & TAMAM) Death to Arabs!

AIESHA: Why do you look at those sites?

ARCHITECT:
To remind myself that every breath I take is a victory,
that the reason I work so hard at architecture

CHORUS: (DELILAH & TAMAM)
and drive myself to the point of collapse

ARCHITECT: is so I will one day create a work that defies
gravity itself.
I think, maybe, if I work hard enough.
and create something worthwhile, something of value.

CHORUS: (DELILAH & TAMAM) Something!

ARCHITECT: It will make people think we are just as
smart, just as human,

CHORUS: (DELILAH & TAMAM) we exist,

ARCHITECT: we matter.
Then, I remember I can't control what people will think.
But I can point to the buildings I'll make and ask,
"Do you want to be remembered
as the murderers of people
who make things like that?
Ask yourself."

CHORUS: (DELILAH & TAMAM) Answer me!

ARCHITECT: I go to those websites and check for
updates to see what I am up against and sometimes I
see stories like yours that read
"Palestinian female suicide bomber's only victim is one
of her own kind."
They show your picture and they show hers,
because they think its funny.
She was a little Palestinian girl

AIESHA: I didn't mean to kill her.
I wanted to kill an enemy.
You can't look at the specifics
of my particular life
in order to understand why I did it.
Others around me had lived more terrible lives
and still wanted to live.
All I knew was that I couldn't breathe.

CHORUS: (DELILAH & TAMAM) No one hears our cries.

AIESHA: I can't breathe.

CHORUS: (DELILAH & TAMAM)
No control over our own destiny

AIESHA: I can't breathe, and, if I can't breathe,
then no one should be allowed to breathe easy.
But, when the time came, I was scared.
I was so scared.
I intended to get a crowd
but

CHORUS: (DELILAH & TAMAM) Timing is everything.

AIESHA: The group I was leaning towards suddenly
moved away
at the same second
I detonated myself.
They knew to get away, all except for this little girl with
big black eyes
and a heavy key around her neck.

CHORUS: (DELILAH & TAMAM)
She couldn't have been more than nine.

ARCHITECT: The website said seven.

AIESHA: Her mother took her with her across hours and
hours of Israeli checkpoints,
so she could work as a maid.

CHORUS: (DELILAH & TAMAM) Her mother was proud.

AIESHA: The women in the refugee camp thought she
was arrogant.
She never let them forget she was once

CHORUS: (AIESHA, DELILAH & TAMAM)
the richest girl in her town.

AIESHA: The town of Ras Abu Ammar.

CHORUS: (DELILAH & TAMAM)
The town that no longer exists.

AIESHA: Have you heard of it?

ARCHITECT: Of course.

AIESHA: It was the place this woman once lived in
before her family fled to Gaza.
She's only allowed to get near her town with a worker's
permit.

CHORUS: (DELILAH & TAMAM)
She's only allowed to go back to be the maid.

AIESHA: She was proud.
She named her only daughter Amal.

CHORUS: (DELILAH & TAMAM) It means hope.

ARCHITECT: And she felt hope

AIESHA:
as she hung the heavy key of the door to the house
she once lived in
around her only daughter's neck.
It didn't matter that the house no longer stood there.
It was her house.
Her daughter would know that—

CHORUS: (AIESHA, DELILAH & TAMAM)
she had a house.

AIESHA: The mother hated to make her daughter
watch her clean toilets.
She hated it even more that day,
because her daughter offered to help
and, even though she said no, Amal took a dripping
brush in her hand.
Amal's mother slapped her.

(TAMAM and DELILAH clap their hands once)

AIESHA: The mother thinks to herself as she watches
her daughter trying to swallow her tears.

CHORUS: (DELILAH & TAMAM)
When my daughter grows up and can understand,
I will apologize for that.

AIESHA:
She imagines how she will one day tell her daughter
Everything one cannot say with a mop in your hand
and work to be done

CHORUS: (AIESHA, DELILAH & TAMAM)
before the curfew is called.

AIESHA: But, years later, the mother
will still *be* sorry,
not just say or feel or act it,

CHORUS: (DELILAH & TAMAM)
but become sorrow itself.

AIESHA: She imagines when Amal is sixteen or so,
they will be laughing.
Her mother will look at her and ask—

CHORUS: (DELILAH & TAMAM) Do you remember that
time I slapped you for no good reason?

AIESHA: Amal will shake her head as if to say

CHORUS: No, I don't remember. (TAMAM)
No, that didn't happen. (DELILAH)
No. (AIESHA, DELILAH & TAMAM)

AIESHA: And Amal's mother will tell her.
You did not deserve that.
Is it possible for you to see that as something I did once,
not someone who I was?

CHORUS: (DELILAH & TAMAM) Amal will nod

AIESHA: And the mother of hope
will know that she taught her daughter the most
important lesson,
the lesson you have to learn

to survive this life with your humanity intact.
She taught her daughter

CHORUS: (AIESHA & ARCHITECT) how to forgive.

AIESHA: It's not something Amal's mother normally
allowed.
But on that day, she sent her outside with the Israeli
teenager of the house,
who doted on her...

CHORUS: (AIESHA, DELILAH & TAMAM)
Look at those big black eyes.

ARCHITECT: The teenager and her friends bought Amal
a falafal sandwich,

AIESHA: because what else do you feed little Arab
children?
Amal saw the janitor at the shop was Palestinian.
She smiled at him,
so he would recognize that she was one too.
The man didn't smile back.
Amal thinks to herself as she takes the first bite of her
falafal sandwich.
When I grow up...

CHORUS: (DELILAH & TAMAM)
I will remember what it's like to be a child.

AIESHA: When I grow up...

CHORUS: (DELILAH & TAMAM)
I will greet children as if they are people.

AIESHA: When I grow up and have children...

CHORUS: (DELILAH & TAMAM)
if people don't greet them, I won't speak to them either.

AIESHA: Amal thinks the sandwich the teenager gave
her was lousy,
not enough parsley.
But she didn't want to hurt her feelings.

so she thanked her
and forced herself to eat it.

ARCHITECT: The teenagers bought her an ice cream cone.

AIESHA: And they ran and left her for dead when they
saw me coming.
I don't think they meant to, but that's what they did.
It was too late to stop everything,
the one step I took back was my last.
The little girl didn't understand she was going to die.
She smiled at me.

ARCHITECT: The last image I had in my mind
before I died was of her picture next to yours.
And underneath it were the words
Finally, they are killing one another.
I thought to myself— will they put my picture next to
the man who ran past my row?
Under our pictures, will they write the words...

CHORUS: (ARCHITECT, DELILAH & TAMAM)
Finally, they are killing one another.

TAMAM:
So, the reason the martyrs don't want you in there

DELILAH: is because you're no good at being no good.

ARCHITECT: No. That is no room for martyrs.
Or maybe it is?
We won't know till we go in that door.
But we can't believe what we've been told.
This can't be heaven.
Heaven is not a place where people segregate
themselves
according to religion or race.

TAMAM: We're in Hell.
Hell is a place where we have to look for the ones we
lost.

DELILAH: No. Earth.
Earth is a place where—there is a door— where no one
who goes in comes out.

AIESHA: No, this is heaven.

CHORUS: Heaven is not a place where people don't
know the answers. (TAMAM)
Heaven is not a place you have to be convinced that
you're in. (DELILAH)

AIESHA: You know a lot about what heaven is not,
But you don't know what heaven is.
The only thing real is that door.

ARCHITECT: You don't know what's beyond it.
I don't believe you've ever been inside.
If you don't spend your life asking hard questions,
you spend your eternity with no answers.
I believe you've been standing here and distracting us
from moving forward

CHORUS: (ARCHITECT, DELILAH & TAMAM)
You keep people here!

ARCHITECT:
I believe each of the groups of women here has
Someone like you,

DELILAH: Someone from their own race,

TAMAM: Someone they feel they can trust,

AIESHA: Someone who keeps them in line
for their own sakes.
You want real answers,
First ask harder questions.
Or you can stay here
and stay safe with me

ARCHITECT: spending an eternity, separate from other
people, asking easy questions like:
Aren't they just a little different?

TAMAM: Am I supposed to feel sorry for what my great-grandparents did before I was born?

DELILAH: Isn't the only way we can assure we're never oppressed is to oppress other people?

ARCHITECT: Wouldn't they do the same to us the minute they had the chance?

CHORUS: (ARCHITECT, DELILAH & TAMAM)
Why is violence only wrong when we use it?

CHORUS: (All four women)
Isn't violence the only thing these people understand?

AIESHA: For your own safety, I keep you asking the wrong questions

CHORUS: (ARCHITECT, DELILAH & TAMAM)
So, we'll stay with you.

ARCHITECT: Instead of going on the quest to find the answer to the only question.

AIESHA: How do you survive in a violent world and not be violent?

CHORUS: (ARCHITECT, DELILAH & TAMAM) Key word

AIESHA: Survive.

ARCHITECT: This place feels too much like limbo.
I've been limbo in all my life.
I'll go first, you two can follow.

AIESHA: You'll be harmed.

ARCHITECT: You don't know that.

AIESHA: Neither do you.

ARCHITECT: Are you two coming or not?

(Pause)

DELILAH & TAMAM: No.

ARCHITECT: (To AIESHA) Then, you come with me.

AIESHA: I'm not allowed in there.

ARCHITECT: Who says?

AIESHA: I say.
What I did was right.
I'm not going to any place where I might have to
question that.

ARCHITECT: Do you know why I keep searching?
What I need to tell the man who murdered me is that
'They rate our lives at nothing,
when we kill ourselves in the hope of hurting them,
we show that we agree,
that we feel our lives are dispensable.

AIESHA: *Our* lives?!
He's going to laugh at you.
What have you suffered?
Did someone make fun of your parents' accents?
Didn't get an award or two because of racism?

CHORUS: (AIESHA, DELILAH & TAMAM) Poor you!

AIESHA: Live my life on earth
in my dirty, crowded refugee camp
in the place that your parents abandoned.

Spend one day
Live like that for one day
knowing that the people

CHORUS: (AIESHA, DELILAH & TAMAM) you love most

AIESHA: have no choice
but to live like that
every second of their living lives.
Then, see if you think limbo
is the only honest place to be.
I am no privileged little

CHORUS: (AIESHA, DELILAH & TAMAM) hypocrite.

AIESHA: You can go around searching for heaven,
I wasn't born to have that luxury.
Maybe that door is back to Earth.
Who knows?

Maybe you and me would return there together.
Maybe then we could see
which of us does any good?

Down there I didn't even have the chance to ask
who makes more of a difference,
in the long run

CHORUS: (DELILAH & TAMAM)
Artists or militants?

AIESHA: People like me or people like you?
Because I never had the chances
you had to do anything different
than what I did.
So don't you judge me.
I don't get to make pretty drawings and such...
and pray people
will maybe look
and maybe see
and maybe think of me as human.
No.

CHORUS: (AIESHA, DELILAH & TAMAM) I am human.

AIESHA: I will be treated as such.

CHORUS: (AIESHA, DELILAH & TAMAM) Or else.

ARCHITECT:
My life and what I do with it is worth something.

AIESHA: Because you had a life worth living.

ARCHITECT: I can't stay here in limbo.
I've been in limbo all my life.
I have to tell the man who killed me—
Hands, movement, change.

CHORUS: *(AIESHA, DELILAH & TAMAM)*
(Chanting together and seeming to ignore the ARCHITECT *as she heads toward the exit)*
Here I only have unanswered questions.
Because, there, l only had unquestioned answers.

Unanswered questions,
unquestioned answers.
I do someone good dead.
I do someone dead good.
What is the point of the revolution that begins with the little hand?
Any little hand?
(Each woman lifts her right hand and looks at it) This little hand?
Unanswered questions,
Unquestioned answers.
I do

(The ARCHITECT *exits.)*

TAMAM: *(At the same time)*   AIESHA & DELILAH:
no one   someone

(AIESHA and DELILAH *look at* TAMAM. *Then, all three women resume chanting together again.)*

CHORUS: *(AIESHA, DELILAH & TAMAM)*
good dead.
I do

DELILAH: *(At the same time)*   AIESHA & TAMAM:
no one   someone

(AIESHA and TAMAM *look at* DELILAH.*)*

CHORUS: *(AIESHA, DELILAH & TAMAM)* dead good.
What is the point of the revolution that begins with the little hand?
Any little hand?
(Each woman lifts her right hand and looks at it) This little hand?

(DELILAH *and* TAMAM *look at one another.*)

DELILAH & TAMAM:
The point is

DELILAH: it pushes,

TAMAM: forces,

DELILAH & TAMAM:
the big hand forward!

TAMAM: With enough movement,

DELILAH & TAMAM:
the times will change.
Little hands, enough movement,

AIESHA: times change.

CHORUS: (AIESHA, DELILAH *&* TAMAM)
Hands, movement, change.
Wait!

(They do not move.)

END OF PLAY

ARCHITECTURE

NOTE

I have included a one-act play based on the same
character as the Architect in THE BLACK EYED.
In the summer of 2002, I met and collaborated with
the director Sam Gold on a workshop production of
ARCHITECTURE at the Hangar Theater Lab. Since
that time, there have been a number of college
productions of ARCHITECTURE.

CHARACTERS & SETTING

THE ARCHITECT, *a woman*
CHORUS, *one to three women*

The stage is very sparse.

.

(*The* CHORUS *in onstage as the lights go up. The*
ARCHITECT *enters.*)

CHORUS:
Tell us who you are and we'll know why you are here.
Tell us who you are and we'll know who you are
looking for.

ARCHITECT: I want to be known only
as the architect of the unseen underlying structures,
and buildings that have never been built.
I'm here for answers from the only one who can give
them to me.

Why must I speak in words when I think in images?
I asked it
while I was on a plane.
I'm on a plane
and it's plain
that the pain
of being on my own plane
is there is a point
where all things intersect.

That point for me is
when I hear a man speaking in Arabic,
And he's heading towards the cockpit.
I understand what's going to happen

CHORUS: —before anyone else does.

ARCHITECT:
Why must I speak in words when I think in images?

I'm an architect of unseen structures
and buildings that will never be built.
I am the mother of children who will never be born.

CHORUS: The lover of men who will remain unloved.

ARCHITECT:
Or rather men who are loved beyond compare,
but will never know it.

CHORUS:
Or how their lives would be changed if they did.

ARCHITECT: It was all the Half-Breed's fault.
I had to meet that son of a bitch who killed me—
It all started with a job interview.
He had an Arab last name.

CHORUS: Half-Breed.

ARCHITECT: I was always falling for the half-breeds.
I can even see him in front of me now.
(Addresses the Half-breed as if he's in front of her)
I walked into your office, Half-Breed
applying for an assistantship.
I read all about you in *Architectural Digest*.
Your daddy's Palestinian.
And your mama's

CHORUS: white.

ARCHITECT: You're a

CHORUS: son of bitch

ARCHITECT: with that side way smile,
that you flash when I walk in.
You were discussing Gehry's new museum with your
minions.

CHORUS: Nice as hell

ARCHITECT: you were,
asking me what I thought of the new museum,

as if my opinion mattered
as if I mattered...
You were polite

CHORUS: too polite

ARCHITECT: to someone applying to be an assistant.
And everyone in the room knew it.
Sidelong glances, and smirks from your minions
He's at it again, their eyes say.

CHORUS: I'm at it again

ARCHITECT: Your eyes say.
I'm glad you asked me.
Architecture is the only thing I can be articulate about.
"I think Gehry's work is over..."

CHORUS: Your eyes never leave mine as your head
cocks to one side.

(Other actors cock their heads to the left.)

ARCHITECT: "...indulgent..."
I meant to say rated.
I think to myself.
Your eyes still don't leave mine
as your head cocks to the other side.

(Actors cock their heads to the right.)

CHORUS: "Why do you say that?"

ARCHITECT: The answer is you make me nervous.
You make me say over-indulgent when I meant
overrated.
If you didn't, I'd still be articulate
about the one thing I can be articulate about.
If that flash in your eyes wasn't signaling.

CHORUS: We don't have to be here.
You and I.
We could, in fact, be somewhere else.

ARCHITECT: —while your lips are asking me...

CHORUS: How would you do it?

ARCHITECT: If I was articulate, I'd say

CHORUS: "hire me and find out."

ARCHITECT: But I'm not so I pull out the drawing
I happen to have,
the draft I made on the train coming over,
You see I do little projects.

CHORUS: I take the requirements and dimensions

ARCHITECT: —that clients give to uninspired and
overrated white men like Gehry to make a museum.

and make my own drawings
of how I would do it

CHORUS: if someone gave me a chance.

ARCHITECT:
And on the ride over to meet you, Half-Breed.
I happened to be working on
my version of the museum
you and your minions—in your jealousy—were
denigrating.

CHORUS: An exercise

ARCHITECT: you might say, if you didn't know
how desperate I get on trains.
I have what I call....

CHORUS: Day-mares.

ARCHITECT: Every time I step on a train, I think
what if

CHORUS: what if

ARCHITECT: what if
I'll always be stuck in this place

where no one is allowed to talk to one another
while trying to get to a place where people do.
So I take out a piece of paper and sketch
and scrap and sketch again.
I never show the work I do on trains to anyone,
why I gave it to you,

CHORUS: God only knows.

ARCHITECT: You appraise it, the way you appraise
everything in your path,
including me in my well-tailored suit.
Noting the flaws and where I wind up wanting,
but startled by the fact that what I've shown you is—

CHORUS: Not bad.

ARCHITECT: If you were to touch me, Half-Breed,— I
would pull out handfuls of your hair.

CHORUS: Not against

ARCHITECT: But towards me.
I can already feel how your hands
will work...

CHORUS: Sculpt.

ARCHITECT: Grasp,
fingers full of my flesh
like clay in your arms.
I'll want to tell you
"It's like you're shaping me!

CHORUS: You're shaping me!"

ARCHITECT: But I'm not articulate, so I'll probably just—

CHORUS: —pant.

ARCHITECT: I'm thinking all this while you are—still
staring at my draft, my exercise.

CHORUS: Buying time.

ARCHITECT: Even though there might be none for sale.

I would marry you in a second. —And, though
half-breed that you are—our children will have an Arab
last name— and I will raise them in the culture you do
not know— and you will not understand why I'm still a
virgin at thirty.

CHORUS: My father's tongue is not my mother tongue

ARCHITECT: is what you'd probably say if I asked you if
you spoke Arabic.
I don't speak hardly a lick of the language either,
but I understand the morsels that count.
My parents never insisted on me speaking back to them.
Took it for granted I would know what they knew.

CHORUS: But I didn't.

ARCHITECT: You will not understand
that the only thing you've got going for you is
you have a chance of understanding
the two languages
I was born to learn and love.

CHORUS: Arabic and architecture.

ARCHITECT: My first-closest-thing-to-a-real-love-affair
involved a man who only knew one.

CHORUS: Arabic.

ARCHITECT:
A mother brought her son to church to see me.
It was the forty day memorial for the grandmother that
I was named after.
He was Lebanese, but born here like me.
But, unlike you, Half-Breed, he knew how things
worked.
His mother had spied me at the seven day memorial,
researched me and my entire family tree.
Mothers love me for their sons.

CHORUS: They mistake inarticulacy for submissiveness.
I soon teach them the difference.

ARCHITECT:
And he came up to me while I was serving coffee
and cups of sweetened grain and candy.

CHORUS: Our fingers touched...

ARCHITECT: as I handed him a cup.
We spoke.
He said...

CHORUS: I wanted to let you know of a scholarship for
Arab female architects. It's an enormous sum of money.

ARCHITECT: Really? How come I haven't heard of it?

CHORUS: Well, it's been fairly recently established.
Today, actually, because it is the first day I've met you
and fallen in love.
I've decided to establish this scholarship
for beautiful young Arab architects.
All you have to do is marry me.

ARCHITECT: That's no scholarship, I thought.
But I was intrigued nevertheless.

He was studying to be a surgeon of the heart,
and it's so fucking bourgeois of me.
It's such a moment of intersection where I don't know
if these are my thoughts
or ones that my mother planted in my head,
but...

CHORUS: I've always wanted to marry a doctor.
and how cute is it that he fixes hearts.

ARCHITECT: And before I know it.
I'm engaged.
It's Easter Sunday.
Christ has risen, and I'm eating brunch.
I'm there with his family and him

at the top of the tallest building in the city.
and everyone is trying to "correct" my Arabic.

CHORUS: Rid me of my Palestinian accent in the few
Arabic words I do know.

ARCHITECT: His father spears a tomato and holds it in
front of my face.
He asks me—

CHORUS: What is this? Say it in Arabic.

ARCHITECT: And I look at him
and he knows that I know what
he's saying.
You see Palestinians and Lebanese pronounce words
differently.
Sometimes it feels like a whole different language.

CHORUS: *(Sing-song)*
Palestinians say tomato, Lebanese say tomoto.
Tomato, tomoto.
Potato, patata.

ARCHITECT: So, during the civil war in Lebanon,
when Lebanese soldiers cornered someone who was
alone
and wanted to find out

CHORUS: (Menacing) Are you a Palestinian? Are you?

ARCHITECT: They'd show him a tomato.
and ask the poor soul

CHORUS: What is this?

ARCHITECT: And if he said tomato instead of tomoto.
They'd know he was a Palestinian and...
(Cocks her hand like a gun, points at audience) Bang!

CHORUS: Let's call the whole thing off.

ARCHITECT: So I'm staring at the face of this man
who no laws are going to make any form of a father
to me,
This is a moment where I longed to be articulate.

CHORUS: But there is safety in silence

ARCHITECT:
His wife took the fork out of the his hand and told him

CHORUS: Be quiet.

ARCHITECT: I know the point of all this was his father
had to let me know

CHORUS:
You will say things the way I want you to. Or else.

ARCHITECT: I looked at the boy I intended to marry,
who with his eyes downcast made it clear.
he knew what his father was doing.
he wasn't defending me.
He couldn't stand up to his father even when he was
wrong
For me.

CHORUS: For you.

ARCHITECT: For me.
That wasn't the main reason why I ended the
relationship,
it was only the point in time that I realized I probably
would.

CHORUS: The scholarship had fine print you didn't read.
It says there is a risk that your first commission is your
last.

ARCHITECT: So I didn't marry that man and waited for
real scholarships, real commissions.

CHORUS: And when they didn't come?

ARCHITECT: I still wasn't sorry. Most of the time.

My second-closest-thing-to-a-real-love-affair involved a
man who spoke the other of the two languages I was
born to learn and love.

CHORUS: Architecture.

ARCHITECT: My current boss.
You know him, don't you, Half-Breed?
He's your rival
in more ways that one.
His name is just under mine on my resume next to the
exercise
you haven't looked up from since I handed it to you.
I was hoping that you'll hire me, Half-Breed,
so I can never see him again.
Not because I don't like him, but because I do.
He was the first man that hired me out of school
He said he believed in me, that my work was

CHORUS: Exceptional.

ARCHITECT: Men lie about such things

CHORUS: when it suits them.

ARCHITECT: But I didn't know that then.
I would never tell a person their work is good when it's
not.
That's the only time it's useful that I'm so inarticulate.
I had a drink with him in his office after a big project

CHORUS: Happy.

ARCHITECT: We discussed my work on it.
My contributions.
His wife called. He told her he was working on a project
and would be home late.

CHORUS: But the project was over.

ARCHITECT:
I know. We continued talking about my work.

Then his colleague came in without knocking and gave
me

CHORUS: the eye.

ARCHITECT: I didn't know what to do with it.
The eye was seeing and signaling

CHORUS: You're at it again.

ARCHITECT: to my boss who smiled back as if to say

CHORUS: I'm at it again.

ARCHITECT: I realized there was a joke being made
and I was somehow

CHORUS: the butt

ARCHITECT: of it.
So I took off hastily.
I left the two men

CHORUS: smiling at each other.

ARCHITECT: I was running away from the woman I was
about to become.
It looks like I haven't run far enough,
because I am here
asking you, Half-Breed
for a job,
a chance.
I live with my parents

CHORUS: always have

ARCHITECT:
always will till a man takes me from my father's house.
You don't understand that concept either, Half-Breed,
staring at my work which you know is original.

CHORUS: Perhaps even better than yours?

ARCHITECT:
I don't need people to tell me I'm talented anymore.

And it's a good thing too, because no one ever does.
There you are, my lovely Half-Breed.

CHORUS: Buying time.

ARCHITECT: Though I don't intend to sell.
Half-Breed!
Can I explain why if you want me
it's important your people come to my home on the day
we marry,
so that you know I do not come from nothing?
The bejeweled old peacock women of my clan
who you pray I won't look like in forty years,

CHORUS: though I'd be proud to have half the strength
and serenity of the least of them.

ARCHITECT: will come to my house to make their
presence known.
to trill and clap, but really to show you
that if you hurt me...
these bejeweled old women
can fly up like birds and peck out your eyes.

What they're saying by showing up to my house early,
witnessing your people escort me from it
is
we are watching...

CHORUS: If you fuck with her, you fuck with us.

ARCHITECT: But you won't know our customs,
Half-Breed!
Your mother wasn't Arab.

CHORUS: Mothers teach their children early
the customs and morals and superstitions that stick.

ARCHITECT: My mother always told me

CHORUS: Marry an Arab man. They have a little sense
of decency.

ARCHITECT:
She means they don't often abandon their families.
My mother thinks if a man doesn't leave you,
that means he loves you,

CHORUS: in the way men know how to love.

ARCHITECT:
I would marry you in a heartbeat, Half-Breed,
and hope you learned how to be a man from your
father.

CHORUS: I have designs on your heart.

ARCHITECT: But I don't know how to execute them.

Why can't love be as easy as architecture?
Why should I have to weigh each word
and place them
as carefully as the next card
in the houses of them
that I used to make incessantly as a child?
What's the point of building something so fragile?

CHORUS: There's too much pressure,
too many forces working against you.

ARCHITECT: That's what is so grave about gravity.
Everything moves in one direction.
Why can't love be as easy as architecture?
Half-Breed, you like me and I like you.

I wish I could just show you
a draft of the nest I would build for us,
with a room for each child I want to have.
Bedrooms all the same size, ours and theirs,
a house with no master bedroom.
A house with no masters.
The only thing I'll have to say is...

CHORUS: Do you like this house? Just say yes or no.

ARCHITECT:
And you will understand my question to mean

CHORUS:
Do you want to live here with me forever? Yes or no.

ARCHITECT: Put the plans in motion or no.
Lay down the first twig of our nest in the nook of a tree
that won't be felled...

CHORUS: —or no.

ARCHITECT:
All this I think of as I look at you looking at my draft.
You clear your half-bred throat.

CHORUS: Ahem.

ARCHITECT: The job interview isn't over.
You haven't looked up from my draft,
but the bell for the minions to leave has been sounded.
I stare at you, Half-Breed.
And from the time it takes you to lift your eyes
from the page to mine,
this is what I think on...

CHORUS: Will our children have your black eyes or my
doe ones?

ARCHITECT:
I think of how I will stop making drafts on subways,
because I want our youngest son to recite for me his A
B Cs and 1 2 3s.

CHORUS: He's not
as quick as his sister.

ARCHITECT: Our daughter who is so arrogant already.
Just like me.

CHORUS: Arrogance is confidence that is snuffed out,
resuscitated,
and is never quite the same again.

Weaker and meaner.

ARCHITECT: Unrecognizable.

CHORUS: Arrogance is what happens to a confident girl
when the whole world, or even just her mother,
tells her that she's nothing and she finds out
she's really something.

Really something.

ARCHITECT:
It's no big tragedy that I rarely sketch anymore
It's my choice, really.
You tell me to get a nanny.

CHORUS: If you want to...

ARCHITECT: As if what I want ever has anything to do
with what I get.
I want to slice myself in half,
so I can keep half for my work.
If I can't do that, I choose my children.
I must raise them.
They must know
that the arms that hold them would die for them.

But that's too difficult to articulate so I tell you

CHORUS: I don't want to.

ARCHITECT: Men like Gehry and you, Half-Breed
Husband, design museums
that have unexceptional collections but are famous
because of

CHORUS: the homes that house them.

ARCHITECT: I wipe asses,
because they are the most beautiful perfect little asses
imaginable,
and no would *wipe them the way I do*!

I content myself with helping you,
showing you where you falter, and you falter often
enough.

CHORUS: It's not sound. It's not sound,
and it's being built a fault line.
Was your head up your ass when you did this?!
Or was it up someone else's?

ARCHITECT: But I can't say that.
I'll have to be vague and suggest

CHORUS: A reinforcement or two.

ARCHITECT: I have to be careful not to bruise your ego.

CHORUS:
Because we all know what happens when that happens.

ARCHITECT: You have your women,
but you never leave me,
That's cold comfort
and I'm in the winter of my life.

CHORUS: But it's comfort just the same.

ARCHITECT: I'm the cement holding your life together,
You pour me, I fit the mold, and I stay there.
Until I crack.
I'll smile softly when I overhear them saying about
me—

CHORUS: She's an architect in her own right too.

ARCHITECT: In my own right, they will say,
which always makes me think,
my relationship with you makes

CHORUS: what is my right

ARCHITECT: somehow in question.

CHORUS: Why must one speak in words when she
thinks in images?

ARCHITECT: Now the last minion steps out.
You've sent them away without a word, Half-Breed.
You lift your head from my page,
weighing your words so carefully
you can't come up with ones.

CHORUS: Welcome to how I feel all the time.

ARCHITECT: Your eyes finally meet mine.
You tilt you head so slightly again.

(CHORUS *cocks their head to the left side.*)

ARCHITECT: look at me sideways
and smile

CHORUS: I can make you fall in love with me

ARCHITECT: but I'll never feel secure in that love.
I know that, if I encourage you, twenty years

CHORUS: from now

ARCHITECT: I will be sitting on the toilet
in a hotel ballroom
on a night you get some award
for a project I did at least half the work on.
Two girls will enter,
about the age I am now,
and one will be bragging in a sing-song voice to the
other...

CHORUS:
"I did it with him again on Sunday. In his office."

ARCHITECT:
She won't have to say his name for me to know,
which him she's singing about.
My Half-Breed Husband!
My mind will flip back to Sunday afternoon
when you said...

CHORUS: I'm going to the office to finish up the project
I'm working on.

ARCHITECT: Sunday is my day.
You take the children and I do my work.
But I don't insist, you usually give me my Sundays.
I don't complain, because the one time I tried.
You told me

CHORUS: Give me a fucking break.
Whose work pays the bills? Who pays the bills?

ARCHITECT: I don't cost much to feed nowadays.
You're a big fat motherfucker now.
I weigh much less than the day you married me
because I have to stay
thin,
gaunt,
hollow.

CHORUS: Take up less space.
Take up less space

ARCHITECT:
I stay thin so no one can say that I'm not trying!

CHORUS: to be in control.
Stay in control.
Who pays the bills?

ARCHITECT: If I was articulate, I would say
"I do".
I organize every aspect of your life
so you can do your life's work.
But I know that's not what you mean.

Most people ask for one day of rest, I beg for one day of
work
and you

CHORUS: Can't give it to me!

ARCHITECT: But I don't complain on that Sunday
and you go to work on

CHORUS: your project

ARCHITECT:
and that was the day I slapped my daughter hard
across the face for the first time.

(All four actors making a slapping sound at the same time.)

ARCHITECT: She gave me a look that said—

CHORUS: I did not deserve that.

ARCHITECT: I will not forget that you did that to me and
I didn't deserve it.

CHORUS: Not even the day you die.

ARCHITECT: That was last Sunday.
I step out of the toilet.
and make my way to the table of

CHORUS: honor.

ARCHITECT:
You smile when our eyes meet from across the room.
I think what you told me on the way over here—

CHORUS: My wife's still a pretty woman.
It's not a boast, it's a fact.

ARCHITECT: I smiled stiffly.
I hate it when people talk about me in front of me in
third person.
Like the client we had over last week who,
when I

CHORUS: stood to serve

ARCHITECT: dessert, he said to you

CHORUS: You've got a regular geisha girl, don't you?

ARCHITECT: I think he meant

CHORUS: harem girl.

ARCHITECT: But he said

CHORUS: geisha girl.

ARCHITECT: But if the difference doesn't matter to him,
why should it matter to me?
I even smiled, thought it was a kind of compliment.
It's been many years since I thought of myself as

CHORUS: a girl.

ARCHITECT: I sit next to you.
You can tell I'm upset.

CHORUS: Everyone can tell. You cock...

ARCHITECT: ...your head to the side,
questioning at first

CHORUS: What's wrong, honey?

ARCHITECT:
Then you see the look in my eyes, you don't ask again
You...

CHORUS: Let it go.

ARCHITECT: And when I ride in silence on the way home
and slam the door behind me
I say out loud, something articulate,
something that's been crystallizing in my mind
since practically the day I met you.
"I just want you to know,

CHORUS: you son of a white bitch,

ARCHITECT: without me, you might be something
but you wouldn't be much."

I'll tell myself to just lighten up and get over it.

CHORUS: There are people dying in Palestine.

ARCHITECT:
And I very easily could have been one of them.
In marriage, there are worse crimes than infidelity.

CHORUS: He still falls asleep stroking your cheek.

ARCHITECT: I now even think it's endearing that he is jealous of my work,
that he needs all my time and attention when he's home.

CHORUS: Like a child

ARCHITECT:
Soon enough, I'll be staring at you in your coffin.
Our three-quarter breed children will be crying...

CHORUS: Baba!

ARCHITECT: Because I made our three-quarter breed children use the Arabic words for family members. Always. They'll be screaming...

CHORUS: Excuse me, would you like to go somewhere and have *(Pause)* coffee?

ARCHITECT:
Your question interrupts my thoughts, Half-Breed.
It startles me.
I didn't realize you were done looking at my exercise and holding it out for me to take back.

I think to myself—
Why are you talking to me?
Can't you see I'm in the middle of envisioning our future together?
I realize that I've done it again.
In my mind, I planned a whole life

CHORUS: birth, death, and remembrance

ARCHITECT: with a guy
before he even asks me out.
Why does my mind flip a lifetime ahead?

We might go out and not hit it off.

I mean, for God's sake, you could be gay
I could be reading all the signs wrong.
It has happened to me before.

You've just asked me for coffee.
Why am I imagining your funereal
with our children standing before you screaming

CHORUS: Baba!

ARCHITECT: Why am I sure
as I stare into your eyes, trying to decide if I want to
have coffee with you,
that one day I'll be staring at your corpse in your coffin,
thinking a thousand thoughts,
not the least of which will be

"There lies your body. Your flesh, that you valued more
than my heart, my love, our family, and my life.
Let. it. rot!"

(Pause)

CHORUS: I said, would you like to have coffee with me?

ARCHITECT: No! No! No!

CHORUS: Tea?

ARCHITECT: And I decline that too, saying I have to go
right back home.
We worked together for a summer and you're always

CHORUS: polite

ARCHITECT:
but you never offer to quench thirsts with me again.

CHORUS: What does this encounter with a half-breed
have to do with you ending up on a plane,
and seeing an Arab man go up to the cockpit?

ARCHITECT: My contract with the Half-Breed's
company was not renewed.
They said I didn't take direction well.

CHORUS: Five years passed.

ARCHITECT: I stayed friends with his assistant so I could
keep tabs on the Half-Breed.
On my thirty-fifth birthday, I called him.

You see I had promised myself
If I'm not married by thirty-five,
I would stop being precious and just have sex
with a man I wanted to love me,
whether or not he did.

CHORUS: Why thirty-five?

ARCHITECT: Because it's no longer cute
that you're a virgin at thirty-five.

I went to lunch with his assistant that week.
He was away on a business trip
I stole the number of his hotel from his assistant's desk.
When she was in the bathroom.

CHORUS: I called him.

ARCHITECT: I told him my name. He said—

CHORUS: You're the girl who worked as an assistant
that summer,
who walked into the interview
with a plan for a museum,
right?

ARCHITECT:
I want to come see you. I want to come stay with you.

CHORUS: Get on the next flight.

ARCHITECT: And I do so.
I've got two fantasies, day-mares, about flying.

CHORUS: First fantasy that I think of as I'm going
through the security check on my way to see the
Half-Breed.

ARCHITECT: It's totally stupid, okay?
But you've got to understand,
I grew up watching American movies

and so I've got this fantasy.
That I'll be on a flight, okay, and it'll be hijacked by my
people, Arabs.

CHORUS: Sounds stupid.

ARCHITECT: I already admitted it was.
But in my fantasy
I'll hear the shouts first in my mother's tongue
that my mother never bothered to teach me to speak.

And I understand what they're saying:
I realize the power of language—
that being able to listen and understand is a different
kind of articulacy
and one I possess.
Like how I can't speak Arabic, but I can comprehend

CHORUS:
and know what's going on before everyone else does.

ARCHITECT: In my fantasy,
all the men are fit and handsome.
They don't intend to kill anybody.
They've lived lives that would break the hardest of men.
They only want to be heard.
Dramatic music will play.

I will stand up,
perfectly manicured and dressed to the meet the press,
my hair will have obeyed me that day
and be everything that I had no choice but to want to be

CHORUS: Light and straight!

ARCHITECT: I will say in perfect Arabic to the men.

CHORUS: But you can't speak Arabic?

ARCHITECT: This is my fantasy, goddamn it.
And in it, I speak perfect Arabic.
I will stand up
and talk those men out of their plans.

I will tell them—
So what if terror helped bring down apartheid in South
Africa?

CHORUS: So what if the Black Panther Movement got
civil rights workers moving
just a little bit quicker?

So what if the American government supports puppet
leaders
who are corrupt and corrupting in our countries.
and kills hundreds of thousands of us
when those leaders don't do
what they say
when they say it?

ARCHITECT: All that still doesn't make it right to kill.
I would say to them—
You're hijacking this plane full of people who are
ignorant,
who are looking at you and saying—

CHORUS: Why are they trying to hurt me? What kind of
people could do such violent, cruel things?

ARCHITECT: They don't know that it's the kind of people
their government has been doing
just as violent, cruel things to
in their name for generations.

Maybe they don't care.

But they're not worth killing yourself over.
They call us terrorists, they are wrong.
We're too good a people to do such harm.

I would tell them
I am a Palestinian.

I lived like an Arab in America.

I held on to my parents' culture and that of my country
of birth,
even when they were at odds.

I held on.
I even only dated my own kind,
because I wanted someone who understood
the first words my family taught me to mean love.

CHORUS: *Ha-beeb-tea.*

ARCHITECT: Even after I realized,
just because a man knows the right words
doesn't mean that he will say them
and even if he says them,
it doesn't mean that he means them.
I will tell them.

CHORUS: I was never ashamed of who I was.

ARCHITECT: From the time my white teacher ignored it
when a white boy lifted my skirt over my head and
called me

CHORUS: Dirty Arab girl

ARCHITECT: I knew I had to synthesize all the signals
about who I was
in a way
that made me not want to be anything else.
I knew if I was not proud to be a Palestinian,
I could not live a life with dignity.
I knew if I did not love my people, no one would.
I would tell them all this

CHORUS: and more.

ARCHITECT:
And, because I was so articulate in my perfect Arabic,
the plane would touch down safely.
All the Americans in the plane would listen to the
grievances of the
men who were willing to kill and die to be heard.
They would be moved by stories of those they feared.

In fact, they'll refuse to get off of the plane,
until Palestinians are given basic human rights,
Iraqis are not killed so their oil can be stolen,
and the rest of America no longer buys
the fucking hypocritical propaganda
our government

CHORUS: You mean
our media.

ARCHITECT: I mean both.

The people on the plane don't buy the crap
that our leaders try to sell us
about trying to secure women's rights...
having the gall to use women's rights
as an excuse to bomb those women

while being allies

CHORUS: bedfellows

ARCHITECT: with good ole Saudi Arabia
and referring to the oppressive Saudi
royal-pain-in-the-ass regime
as our friends for no other reason than

CHORUS: they give America their juice.

ARCHITECT: When all those conditions are met,
everyone on the plane leaves safely.

There will be a movie made about me.
I would end up on Oprah, telling my story.

CHORUS: I will be articulate

ARCHITECT: One of the audience members will tell me

CHORUS:
Julia Roberts does a great job playing you in the movie.
I'm glad she acknowledged you at the Academy
Awards.
But I've got to say.

We the P T A board members of Lansing, Michigan
think you're even prettier than Julia is.

ARCHITECT: Of course, I'll blush and smile benevolently
and Oprah will say

CHORUS:
More importantly, she's also a brilliant architect.

ARCHITECT:
But she won't have to say "in her own right."

Before the first commercial break,
it'll be clear that Oprah and I are now best friends.
I'll let her announce that I've been commissioned to
design
the new United Nations building
since the old one obviously wasn't engineered to work
right.

CHORUS: It had the master bedroom syndrome.

ARCHITECT: And, in my fantasy, the love of my life

who may or may not be the Half-Breed,
because maybe when my people are no longer under
siege,
no longer a dying breed,
I won't feel I owe it to my people to mate with my own
kind.

I'll be free in the most important way it is to be free.
I'll be free to love who I love.

And, whoever that man who I love is,
he will be sitting in the audience.

Our eyes will connect for the slightest second
We'll remember

CHORUS: We don't have to stay here much longer.
You and I, we will soon go somewhere else.

ARCHITECT: I'll feel a shot of warmth in me,
like a dying fire that with one breath he can keep aglow.

I know that no matter how many faces are in a crowd,
I'll find his.

CHORUS: I'll find his.

ARCHITECT: I'll seek out his gentle eyes in a crowd till
the end of our days
and the last of our nights.
I'll live with the man I love but

CHORUS: I won't need to marry

ARCHITECT: to feel secure in a man's love
and know he'll stay and raise the children we have
together

CHORUS: I won't need to marry

ARCHITECT: to be an honest woman.
I'll be clear that I am.

CHORUS: Or rather I'll be
rich and powerful
enough that categories like that don't apply.

ARCHITECT: Bottom line is, I won't need to marry.
I will be a hero like Doctor King or Gandhi!
But no one shoots me.
(Pause)
Did everyone hear that? No one shoots me.
That's not part of the fantasy I have as I go through the
security check on my way to lose my virginity to the
Half-Breed.
I don't want to die that way.

CHORUS: Does anybody want to die that way?

ARCHITECT: I think what a stupid fantasy that is.
I've clearly been watching too many American movies.
I will refuse to watch the one on the flight.
I think that to myself as I give the girl at the counter my
ticket.

I'm afraid to fly,
though I do it every chance I get.
So much of my life is lived in the space between

CHORUS: Fear and desire.

ARCHITECT: It's kind of funny.
Flying makes me understand the

CHORUS: allure of suicide.

ARCHITECT: I find my seat

CHORUS: and rest like I never rest.

ARCHITECT: You see, I don't work on planes.
It's the one time I don't feel guilty for not working.
The one place where I can just sit here
and let life take me where I'm going.
I think to myself.
If this plane I'm on goes down, at least I won't
have to finish that project I'm working on,
or

CHORUS: wake up

ARCHITECT: sweaty with the knowledge
it is possible that
my ambition overreaches my abilities,
or

CHORUS: face the fact

ARCHITECT:
that I know that the structures I build with my hands
will never be like the ones I see in my head.
Or that I'll die alone.

CHORUS:
Or married to a man who makes me wish I were.

ARCHITECT: If the plane goes down, it'll be a

CHORUS: relief.

ARCHITECT: Mine will be a life full of potential

CHORUS: cut short,

ARCHITECT: rather than a life fully realized and

CHORUS: found wanting

ARCHITECT: I won't have to work or face failure.
But if it were to go down, there is one thing I would regret.
And that lead me to the next fantasy I have while settling in my seat
on a plane
which will take me to the place
where I will lose my virginity to the Half-Breed.
I look for the straps of my seatbelt.
Knowing I'm a beast

CHORUS: animal

ARCHITECT: beast, but to have been a beast with only one back all my life.
To die a virgin!

CHORUS: What a tragedy that would be.

ARCHITECT: Tell me about it.
So my fantasy as I strap my seatbelt on—

CHORUS: Click.

ARCHITECT: —is that if I somehow figure out that this plane is going to crash.
And I realize I'm going to die a virgin.
I'd stomp up to the

CHORUS: cock—

ARCHITECT: pit,
and who says language isn't everything?
And once I get to the

CHORUS: cock—

ARCHITECT: pit,
I'd get on that loudspeaker and say—
Unfasten your seatbelts

CHORUS: Motherfuckers!

ARCHITECT: If this plane is going down,
someone is going down on me!

CHORUS:
But I never have the guts to act out my fantasies.
So even if the plane went down

ARCHITECT: by accident

CHORUS: technical failure instead of the emotional kind.

ARCHITECT: I probably wouldn't not go up to the

CHORUS: cock—

ARCHITECT: pit and say that.
I would have sat in my seat like I

CHORUS: sat in the seat of disbelief.

ARCHITECT: when I actually did hear those men
shouting in Arabic
and it wasn't a fantasy.
It was real.
It was my life.
It was awful.
I knew what they were saying and I knew what they
were doing

CHORUS: before anyone else did.
Though my mother's tongue is not my tongue.

ARCHITECT: One of them passed by my row and I
thought to myself...
as if I was an American with ancestors on the
Mayflower
and had no understanding of America's history
in the Middle East.

I thought to myself—

CHORUS: What kind of person could do such a thing?

ARCHITECT: The one who ran past me who was chubby

CHORUS: like my brothers.

ARCHITECT: Stupid me, thinking—

CHORUS: —inappropriate thoughts.

ARCHITECT: Thoughts that make me thank heaven I am
so inarticulate.

CHORUS: As the man tied up a stewardess....

ARCHITECT: I was thinking I like chubby men.
I don't trust men if they're too thin.

I don't trust men
if they aren't susceptible
to the least pernicious of appetites.

CHORUS: I think you just don't trust men.

ARCHITECT: He passed my row and our eyes met.
Perhaps because I was the only one looking up,
not crying.
He froze.
The way Arabs outside the Arab world do
when they recognize that someone here

CHORUS: is one of my kind.

ARCHITECT: He waited for me to speak
and when I couldn't,
he went on his way without a backward glance.

From the look in his eyes,
I lost all hope that any of us would live.

I took out my sketch book
and sketched for the first time

CHORUS: without fear.

ARCHITECT: I took out my sketch book,
did my work
and saw that it was good.

I'm here to find that man who passed me and knew I
was an Arab.
He's in that room in front of us.
I just know it.

I came here because I couldn't rest.

I couldn't rest
because I knew that I could have stopped him
before he did what he did
if I had the right words

CHORUS: There are no right words.

ARCHITECT: Goddamn it. There are!

CHORUS: Don't blame yourself.

ARCHITECT:
What's the point of being articulate when no one
can hear anything they aren't ready to hear?
It's not about blame.

It's not about blame.
It's about knowing
that there are always words—

CHORUS: Words that work like spells

ARCHITECT: —something you can say
that will stop someone from doing something

CHORUS: awful.

ARCHITECT:
We tell ourselves that there aren't such words,
but that's because we don't
know them.
and probably can't know them,
but it doesn't mean they don't exist.

It doesn't mean I couldn't have used them then.
It's too late

CHORUS: in every sense of the word,
So stay here, become one of us.

ARCHITECT: I can't.
I still need to know what those words are.
I still need to be articulate.
The man who killed me is the only one who can tell me

CHORUS: It's too late.

ARCHITECT: —what those words are.

(The ARCHITECT *takes a step forward. Lights out)*

END OF PLAY